RELIGION
and
POLITICS
in ISRAEL

JEWISH POLITICAL AND SOCIAL STUDIES

General Editors

Steven M. Cohen   Daniel J. Elazar

RELIGION *and* POLITICS *in* ISRAEL

CHARLES S. LIEBMAN
AND ELIEZER DON-YEHIYA

INDIANA UNIVERSITY PRESS

Bloomington

For Rivkah, Ronen, and Ruth
and
Zafrira, Ido, and Yishai

Copyright © 1984 by Charles S. Liebman and Eliezer Don-Yehiya
All rights reserved
No part of this book may be reproduced or utilized in any form
or by any means, electronic or mechanical, including photocopying
and recording, or by any information storage and retrieval system,
without permission in writing from the publisher. The Association
of American University Presses' Resolution on Permissions constitutes
the only exception to this prohibition.
Manufactured in the United States of America

Library of Congress Cataloging in Publication Data

Liebman, Charles S.
  Religion and Politics in Israel.

  (Jewish political and social studies)
  Includes index.
  1. Judaism—Israel. 2. Religion and state—Israel.
  3. Israel—Politics and government. I. Don-Yiḥya,
Eli'ezer. II. Title. III. Series.
BM390.L525   1984   322'.1'095694   83-48172
ISBN 0-253-34497-2
1 2 3 4 5 88 87 86 85 84

Contents

Preface / vii

1. The Meaning of Jewish Identity — 1

2. Separation of Religion and State in Israel: A Program or a Slogan? — 15

3. The "Status Quo" Agreement as a Solution to Problems of Religion and State in Israel — 31

4. The Dilemma of Reconciling Traditional Culture and Political Needs: Civil Religion in Israel — 41

5. Religious Orthodoxy's Attitudes toward Zionism — 57

6. Religious Leaders in the Political Arena — 79

7. The Anatomy of a Religious Party — 100

8. Religious Extremism in Israel — 119

Notes / 138

Index / 145

Preface

There are two presuppositions about religion and politics prevalent in the West in general and in the United States in particular. One is that democratic political systems cannot deal effectively with religious issues. Therefore, the politicization of religion threatens the system's stability. The second is that religion is undermined and corrupted by political involvement.

These presuppositions are built on a number of assumptions, which include the following: First, religious issues are ultimate issues upon which religious advocates cannot compromise. Hence, if religious issues are allowed to penetrate into the political arena, the group holding one point of view will be locked in an irreconcilable conflict with the group holding another point of view, to the detriment of the civil order. Second, religion deals with questions of conscience. Governments ought to maintain strict neutrality in dealing with such matters in order to preserve individual liberty. Third, religion is true to itself only when it persuades its adherents to exercise free choice in the direction it desires. The entry of religion into the political arena means the attempt to invoke the agencies of the state to achieve religious objectives. This state of affairs, it is argued, is counterproductive from a religious point of view, since coercion renders free moral choice impossible. Finally, the temptations of political power and the attainment of a religious group's goals through political action rather than through persuasion, corrupts the religious establishment. In the long run, attachment to the instruments and material rewards of politics leads religion to advocate coercion or to adopt an increasingly materialistic, compromising, and worldly orientation at the expense of spiritual, principled, and other-worldly goals.

There are two problems with these attitudes. First of all, they assume that a certain type of secular-libertarian society is the most desirable. There is much to be said, for example, on behalf of a state that remains neutral or never seeks to coerce its citizens regarding matters of conscience, but one cannot assume that such a state is either possible under some circumstances or desirable under others. We allude to this question in chapter four.[1] Second, although they are true in part, the assumptions we have listed are not absolute truths. Our study of Israel demonstrates that these assumptions are more appropriately formulated as dangers to the polity or religion rather than as the inevitable consequence of mixing religion and politics. Religion in Israel is so directly involved in political life that one cannot understand religious developments there without noting the importance of politics, or study Israeli politics without regard to the role of religious values and religious parties. Nevertheless, Israel is a stable democratic society, and the religious establishment, while hardly uncorrupted, does not appear to have been seriously undermined or its values significantly distorted by virtue of its political involvement.

Admittedly, there are unfortunate consequences for both the stability of the political system and the integrity of religion that result from mixing religion and politics. What our study shows, however, is that this mix may be inevitable in at least certain kinds of societies. In addition, certain benefits may accrue to both religion and the political system—a possibility that the advocates of separating religion and politics would do well to ponder.

What does the study of religion and politics entail? To many it means simply political controversy over religious issues. In the case of Israel, such a study would focus on the issue of whether public transportation should function on the Sabbath, whether marriage and divorce procedures should be in the hands of religious authorities, whether a Jew is to be defined only by religious law or by some other criterion, how much public funding ought to be expended on religious causes or institutions, whether non-Orthodox movements within Judaism ought to receive governmental recognition, etc. Such a study might also focus on religious parties viewed as parties representing the interests of religious voters.

There is, we believe, importance to such studies, and a few of our chapters address themselves to the topic of religion and politics in this manner. But these analyses are only part of a broader picture and, viewed in isolation, are likely to mislead. First of all, they focus attention on religion as a politically divisive issue—as the political interest of one sector of the body politic. Now the Jewish population of Israel is divided over some religious questions, deeply divided. But religion also integrates the population and provides a vehicle for socialization and political legitimation that the focus on religious conflict overlooks. Second, defining religion and politics as the study of religious issues in the public realm omits the important dimension of the interrelationship between religion and politics. The kinds of questions that we see as central to the topic are: What impact, if any, does religion have on politics and politics on religion? What are the consequences for Israeli political culture of Israel's being a Jewish state? What particular consequences flow from the fact that religious Jews organize a political party? Is that party different from other parties by virtue of its commitment to religious values? How does being religious affect one's political perceptions? Our focus is on the interrelationship of religion and politics. Our discussion of specific controversies over religious issues is in the context of this interrelationship. We feel that this approach provides a more realistic assessment of the condition of religion and politics in Israel and offers a framework for comparing that condition with those prevailing in other states.

Preface

The first chapter, "Jewish Identity," provides the foundation for understanding what being Jewish means to nonreligious Israeli Jews. The chapter explains that Jewish identity in Israel, in contrast to Jewish identity in the United States, is primarily national and political. Hence, most Israelis view their national identity as synonymous with and a reinforcement of their Jewish identity. As the second chapter then explains, this national Jewish identity is grounded in a recognizably religious culture, so that virtually all Israeli Jews not only affirm the value of a Jewish state but agree that this entails a relationship between religion and state. What troubles nonreligious Israelis, therefore, is not the fact that the symbols of the state stem from and even point to the religious tradition, or that the state provides support for religious insitutions, or even that there is an absence of freedom of conscience, but that religious legislation often imposes bothersome and inconvenient prohibitions.

Chapter three describes the specific institutional framework, the "status quo" agreement that regulates the relations between religious and nonreligious political interests.

Chapter four notes that despite religion's importance in Israeli political culture, it cannot adequately socialize the population or legitimate the social order among the nonreligious public. Hence, there is a need on the part of the political elite to reformulate the religious tradition. The chapter deals with three major strategies in the reformulation.

Chapter five looks at the religious side of the coin by describing the evolution of religious attitudes toward Zionism and the Jewish state, the different conceptions of Zionism that were held by religious elites, and the development of religious political parties in accordance with these attitudes and conceptions.

Chapter six discusses the relationship between religious leaders and political leaders of both religious and nonreligious parties. Their relative influence and the extent of their autonomy, competition, and interdependence are examined.

Chapter seven is a study of the largest of the religious parties, the National Religious Party. It explores the party's role and the perception of the party among its adherents, the growth of factionalism within the party, and the reasons for the party's recent electoral failure. The reasons, as the chapter shows, have to do in part with the growing consensus regarding religious or quasi-religious values within Israeli society, which weakens the party's hold on its electorate.

The final chapter, devoted to the growth of religious extremism in Israel, demonstrates how, in the last analysis, politics remains a secondary and derivative value to some religiously committed Israelis. However important an influence politics may have on religious values, the alternative of turning against the world, against political reality, against the dynamic of political representation, remains an option, however high its cost. But when these values are, in turn, politicized, one is inevitably left with movements whose presuppositions and aspirations are nondemocratic.

All the chapters in this book are based on articles that the authors have written jointly or individually. We have been collaborating on research in Israeli politics and religion for almost fifteen years. Even those articles that originally appeared under one of our names reflect the suggestions of the other. In preparation of this volume, however, all the articles except that which constitutes chapter four have been rewritten—some so extensively that they barely resemble their previous forms. In all cases we have indicated where the earlier versions appeared.

Our good friend and colleague Steve Cohen offered a number of helpful suggestions in improving the original draft. We are very grateful to Indiana University Press for the careful consideration given our manuscript.

RELIGION *and* POLITICS *in* ISRAEL

− 1 −

The Meaning of Jewish Identity

The question of Jewish identity is a complex one. An absence of good theoretical and empirical material on the subject means that we not only lack authoritative answers to questions concerning Jewish identity; we don't even agree on the proper questions. There are those who discuss Jewish identity, like every other question of contemporary Jewish concern, from the background of European Jewish enlightenment and emancipation in the eighteenth and nineteenth centuries. Others see it in the context of the general problem of identity that confronts contemporary man. Man, in their view, is perplexed by modern society—a technological, bureaucratic, impersonal society that prescribes a variety of different roles and challenges the possibility of any meaningful identity.

Although these approaches contribute to our general understanding of the problem of Jewish identity, we do not think they take us very far. The problem is not so much their highly conjectural nature—many of the assertions in this chapter are no less conjectural—but their broadness. To rephrase the metaphor, they hide the trees by focussing on the forest. Jewish scholars in general might be better advised to pay more attention to the trees; we will attempt to do so in this chapter.

We are interested in Jewish identity in Israel. However, we can better understand its meaning by comparing it with Jewish identity in the United States. Our empirical assertions are based primarily on our own observations. Some of these observations are confirmed in two studies of Israeli Jewish identity by Simon Herman.[1] We also rely on data from our study of civil religion in Israel based in part on a random sample of adult Israeli Jews conducted in December 1975.[2] Our observations conform, in part,

This chapter is a revised version of "The Present State of Jewish Identity In Israel and the United States," by Charles S. Liebman, which appeared in *Forum* (1977).

to some of the empirical studies of American Jews. But we do not pretend that most of what we have to say is grounded in solid empirical findings. Indeed, some of the things we say may elude empirical confirmation.

A second caveat is in order. We are necessarily speaking in generalities. When we talk about Jews in Israel or in the United States we cannot include all Jews. The problem is twofold. First, our statements about Jews are not accurate for every individual who falls into the category "Jew," or even for every subgroup of Jews. Second, we tend, like other writers who discuss large groups of people, to have a certain prototype in mind. The kind of Jew to whom we refer, unless otherwise noted, is of East European origin. If he lives in the United States he is second- or third-generation American, and if he lives in Israel he arrived there by the early 1950s. He is not rigorously observant of traditional Jewish law. In other words, if he lives in Israel he will not call himself or be called by others a *dati*,[3] although he may identify himself as a traditional Jew, and if he lives in the United States he will not be described as an Orthodox Jew.

BASIC QUESTIONS OF JEWISH IDENTITY

There are two questions that we take to be central to the subject of Jewish identity. First of all, how does one define Judaism? What does one mean when one says, "I am a Jew"? What is the subject's understanding of Judaism? Second, how intense is the individual's sense of Jewish identity? How important is Judaism to him? What part does the individual's Jewish identity play in his total self-identity?

The two questions are related but not identical. Obviously, if one person defines Judaism as a pattern of consumptive preferences—that is, he conceives of himself as a Jew because he prefers certain kinds of foods, or a certain type of home, or certain social amenities—and another person conceives of Judaism as encompassing his historical, national, ethnic, religious, political, social, and ethical self-identity, then it stands to reason that the former will be less intensely Jewish than the latter. But even if two Jews agreed that being Jewish is in essence the identification with a group of common symbols pointing to a relationship with the transcendent, or that being Jewish entails a sense of kinship with those who identify themselves as Jews, this conception might be a matter of intense concern and involvement to one of them and a matter of relative indifference to the other. In addition, as our phrasing of the second question suggests, the intensity of one's Jewish identity is also a function of the value assigned to one's other identities. Intense involvement in and fulfillment from an activity that has no Jewish association—whether it is of an occupational, political, or social nature—probably means a diminution of one's Jewish identity, regardless of what one's conception of Judaism might be.

THE DEFINITION OF JEWISH IDENTITY IN ISRAEL

Our discussion will focus on the non-*datiim* (plural of *dati*). They constitute the vast majority of the population, although, as we shall see in later chapters, *datiim* have played an increasingly important role in Israeli public life in recent years, exercising an influence on many non-*datiim*. Various sample surveys have asked Israelis to identify themselves as religious (*dati*), traditional, or secular. As a general rule these surveys have found that fewer than 20 percent of the population define themselves as *dati*; the other 80 percent are split about equally between traditional and secular. Most Sephardic (Oriental) Jews (Jews originating primarily from Islamic countries) fall into the broad category "traditional," which includes those who observe most religious practices as well as those who observe very few. That which distinguishes the traditionalists from the *datiim* is the fact that the former do not necessarily perceive their observance of Jewish law as fulfilling God's commands; rather they see it as a way of maintaining Jewish custom and showing respect for familial tradition. The secularists, most of whom are Ashkenazic (originating from European or other Western countries), also observe many Jewish rites. One survey showed that 38 percent of them reported that they attend a synagogue on the High Holy days, 43 percent that they kept a kosher home, 17 percent that they observed the laws of kashrut outside the home, and 80 percent that they celebrated the Sabbath in some way. What distinguishes traditionalists from secularists is the rigor with which the traditionalists observe whatever it is they do observe, and the fact that their observance is not simply a matter of personal preference or family style but is related to a more general conception of how a Jew ought to behave.

The Israeli Jews upon whom we choose to focus are, by and large, conscious of what religious observance is. They observe at least some of the religious commands but do not view them as personally binding; nor do they regard the lack of observance as "sin," as do the *datiim*. The vast majority of non-*dati* Israelis do affirm a relationship between Judaism and religion. But unlike the *datiim*, they do not find an intense personal meaning in religion. On the contrary, their religious identity is increasingly expressed in the public domain, and its meaning is increasingly associated with public rather than private life.

The day has passed when Zionism was a surrogate for religion. The radical secularists who argued that religious symbols had to be transformed and transvalued to serve the needs of the Jewish people and the Jewish state no longer dominate the cultural and political life of the society. The voice of those who would sever all connections between contemporary Judaism and the religious tradition of the past has certainly been silenced. Therefore, in view of the fact that 93 percent of the adult Jewish population, according to a survey we commissioned in December of 1975, feel that Israel must be a Jewish state, it follows that the majority of Israelis favor some reflection of the religious tradition in Israel's public life. Indeed, as many as 77 percent feel that there ought to be some relationship between religion and state in Israel.[4]

The 1975 survey revealed that to the vast majority of Israelis, a Jewish identity encompasses something besides a religious identity. Religion is an aspect, and may even provide a form and expression, of Judaism but does not represent its basic content. Most Israelis conceive of the Jews as a nation. The sense of a Jewish nationality that entails the obligations and responsibilities that Jews have toward one another is, for many Israelis, the critical aspect of their Jewish identity. Of all the obligations incumbent upon Israel as a Jewish state, her special responsibility to Diaspora Jewry was affirmed by the highest number of respondents (83 percent).

There is an increasing tendency for the Israeli and Jewish identities to overlap and for religious symbols to play an increasingly prominent role in their expression. Simon Herman, in the studies referred to above, has found that the stronger one's sense of Jewish identity, the stronger one's sense of Israeli identity. This attitude is further reinforced by Arab opposition to Israel as a Jewish state and their opposition to a Jewish majority in the land of Israel. It also helps explain why the more nationalistic and militant elements in the Jewish population have increasingly accepted a religious definition of the Jewish right to the land and why religious symbols play an increasingly prominent role in their assertions of national identity.

Jewish Identity and Israeli Identity

The past few years have seen a change in Jewish identity among Israelis in a direction that few would have predicted. There were those who at one time believed that Israelis were developing an identity totally divorced from their sense of Jewishness. Israeli youth in particular, it was felt, had developed a strong Israeli identity, while their Jewish identity was atrophying. George Friedman's *The End of the Jewish People?* first published in 1965, is the best example of this type of thinking.[5] Israelis themselves were fearful of the spread of Canaanism, an ideology that was particularly attractive to young intellectuals in the early years of the state. The Canaanites argued that Israelis must seek their cultural and historical roots among the peoples and civilizations that had lived in the land. The Israeli, they asserted, was not a Jew but the successor to the ancient Semitic, Canaanite, and Hebrew peoples. They favored the dissolution of ties to the Disapora and its history. Although the Canaanites were always a peripheral, numerically insignificant group, the thrust of their cultural and political program—the dissociation of Israelis from the Jewish people and tradition and the adoption of a new Israeli identity—was accepted, to varying degrees, by many Israeli youth, educators, army officers, intellectuals, and, in modified form, by Ben Gurion himself. Ben Gurion articulated a Statist ideology, which stressed the biblical, as opposed to the diasporic, roots of modern Israel. He questioned the Zionist, and by implication the Jewish, commitment of those who chose to remain in the Diaspora rather than come to Israel. Canaanism and Statism converged in an attitude of contempt for the non-Israeli Jew and non-Israeli Jewish culture—an attitude that might ultimately have severed the Israeli Jew from his identity with the Diaspora Jew, and Israeli culture from Jewish culture.

This tendency is probably intrinsic to Israel, but it no longer dominates any of the institutions of the society. There is no better evidence of its failure than the enormous importance accorded to the Holocaust by Israeli society, its schools, the mass media, and the army. Israelis view the state as linked emotionally and spiritually to the Holocaust. Jewish suffering is seen in repeated opinion polls as the greatest legitimation of Jewish rights to the Land of Israel. The Israeli's perception of the Holocaust strengthens his sense of continuity with historical Judaism and reinforces the feeling that Israelis, like the victims of the Holocaust, are isolated and beleaguered because they are Jewish. Israelis also see their condition symbolized by the biblical phrase "a people that dwelleth alone" (Numbers 23:9). The Jewish tradition is thus reinforced by Israel's experience at the same time that it serves to shape the Israelis' perception of their condition and helps them come to terms with it.

Obviously, Israelis also recognize the uniqueness of their condition. They do distinguish, for example, between the fate of the Holocaust victims and their own situation. Many Israelis still harbor the feeling that the Holocaust victims were too passive. Israelis share a belief that if there had been a state there would not have been a Holocaust. But even the distinctions, in this case, contribute to a sense of historical continuity.

What has been taking place among Israelis in the last few years is, as we have suggested, an increasing overlap between their Israeli and Jewish identities. But whereas religious symbols play an increasingly important role in Israeli public or collective life, Judaism has no great significance to the individual in terms of his spiritual and personal self-definition or his behavior. There is no evidence, for example, that the level of religious observance has increased, that more people refrain from violating the Sabbath or eating bread on Passover, or that more people pray.

There are contrary trends, which find their most dramatic expression within the nonreligious kibbutzim. One does find young people who look to religion and the Jewish tradition for personal meaning, to find guidance in their personal lives, to help them relate to the ultimate conditions of their existence. Not all non-*dati* Israelis have abandoned the spiritual quest or the hope of finding answers in Judaism. But for the majority, Judaism touches only the public aspects of their lives.

There is, however, evidence of a growing respect for the religious tradition and an increased stress on the interrelationship between Israel and the Diaspora. Simon Herman reports on a survey of Israeli high-school youth that he conducted in order to compare the relative potency of Israeliness and Jewishness. In 1965 and 1974 he asked students to mark their position on an Israeli-Jewish scale of one to seven, where one is an Israeli identity and seven a Jewish identity. In 1965 the mean position of the entire sample was 3.5, in other words, on the Israeli side. In 1974 is shifted to 4.2, or just beyond the mid-point (4.0) and to the Jewish side. Among those students who defined themselves as *dati,* the shift was from 5.1 to 5.4, among those who defined themselves as traditionalists, it was from 3.6 to 4.4, and among those who defined themselves as secularists, it was from 2.6 to 3.1. Herman's data support his earlier finding that Jewish and Israeli identities are mutually reinforcing. Where they are separated and compartmentalized, the result is a weaker Jewishness and a less-rooted Israeliness. Hence, as might be expected, those who define themselves as *dati* have both a stronger Israeli and a stronger Jewish identity than non-*datiim.* The decline of Jewish identity from the older to the younger generation, which Herman and others have noted, is not unrelated to, and bodes poorly for, the future of Israeli identity. Indeed,

The Meaning of Jewish Identity

to the extent that an identity crisis exists in Israel today, it is a crisis of Israeli, not Jewish, identity; the political elite looks to the Jewish tradition to reinforce loyalty and commitment to the state.

THE INTENSITY OF JEWISH IDENTITY IN ISRAEL

The fusion of Israeli and Jewish identities (a fusion that is not complete nor ever likely to be complete) means that an Israeli identity is not the same as national identities are to the citizens of European countries, and being Jewish is different to Israelis than to Diaspora Jews.

Our identity determines our relationship to others (who I am tells me who the "other" is and hence what my relationship ought to be with him), but our relationship to others also contributes to our identity (how others behave toward me reveals how others see me, which in turn helps determine how I see myself). The outstanding characteristic of Jewish identity in Israel is that precisely because Jews constitute 85 percent of the society, and because the vast majority of Jews mix only with other Jews, their Jewish identity is taken very matter-of-factly. Israeli Jews cannot conceive of themselves as anything other than Jews. As one Israeli youth speaking of herself and her friends once said to us, "My Jewish identity is as much a part of me as my name—but really of no greater consequence." This twenty-two-year-old girl was responding to her experiences with American Jewish youth in Israel whose Jewish concern and commitment quite overwhelmed her. She knew she was Jewish. She would not think of denying her Jewish identity, but, most significantly, she never really thought about her Jewishness. This perspective, we believe, is characteristic of most Israeli-born Jews.

Israelis sometimes use the expression "this Jew" as synonymous not only with "Israeli" but with "man." The expression entered the Hebrew vocabulary from the Yiddish. But in Eastern Europe it had a specific connotation—"one of us." In Israel it loses all its emotional overtones. In other words, the term "Jew" is increasingly devoid of the expressive symbolic meaning that it still possesses in the Diaspora. This phenomenon is to be expected in a country where being Jewish is the natural state of affairs. But the process leads to trivialization of one's Jewishness. No doubt many of Israel's founders would have been pleased by this. It does represent the normalization of Judaism for which early Zionist leaders devoutly wished. It is significant, therefore, that this situation is a cause of concern to many Israelis, particularly the political and educational leaders.

The situation may, in fact, be changing. The increasing overlap between Jewish and Israeli identities has led to an increasing self-consciousness about being Jewish. Even non-*datiim* are interested in Jewish history and in learning more about Judaism, and they do, as we noted, feel a sense of kinship with other Jews.

The Definition of Jewish Identity in the United States

Most American Jews, under the impact of the American environment, conceive of Judaism primarily in religious terms. This generalization has been less true at some times than at others. It is less true today than it was twenty years ago, but by and large most American Jews and most non-Jews think of Judaism as distinct from but structurally comparable to Catholicism and Protestantism. Indeed, until very recently it was only by defining themselves as a religion that Jews could legitimate their separate social and cultural existence.

There has always been a distinct minority of American Jews who define their Jewish identity in cultural, ethnic, and even national terms. Contrary to what one might have suspected twenty years ago, there is no evidence that they are disappearing. Indeed, in the last two decades, ethnic distinctiveness has been legitimized in the United States, largely through the struggles of the blacks. This development has, in turn, legitimated an ethnic Jewish identity. How widespread the legitimation of ethnic distinctiveness is, how consequential it is, or how permanent it is, remains to be seen.

We must be very careful in explicating what Jews mean by a religious self-conception. Paradoxically, the religious definition tends to be more inclusive than an ethnic or cultural one. Those Jews who define themselves as something other than religious tend to do so because they are *not* religious, but Jews who regard themselves as religious do not exclude cultural, ethnic, or even national aspects from their self-conception. This broad definition has not always been accepted; Reform Judaism in the United States was, until about forty years ago, rather exclusivistic in defining the meaning of Judaism.

The greater the religious commitment of the Jew (measured by his religious observance), the higher he tends to score on such measures of Jewish identity as Zionism, traditional belief, Jewish organizational affiliation, and Jewish education.[6] The only measure of Jewish identity that does not correlate well with traditional observance is Jewish associationalism—the number of close Jewish friends one has or the frequency of visiting Jews as compared to non-Jews.

It is rather difficult to specify what precisely the American Jew means when he calls himself or thinks of himself as a religious Jew. Fewer than half of all American Jews are even affiliated with a synagogue. Fewer than a quarter of all American Jews participate regularly in synagogue services, and only about half of them follow some regular pattern of Jewish observance that goes beyond celebrating Passover and Hannukah, holidays that are observed in some form by the vast majority of American Jews. We do not mean the rigorous pattern of Orthodox observance, which probably involves no more than 5 percent of American Jews. We are talking about any regularized observance, such as candle lighting on Friday evening or some pattern of living that recognizes the Sabbath as a distinctive day.

The continued nominal adherence of American Jews to a religious self-conception, coupled with their particular behavior patterns, suggests that while American Jews may conceive of Judaism as a religion, the primary content of that religion is the obligation and responsibility that one Jew has for another. Jewish identity seems to mean above all else membership in the Jewish people and a sense of kinship with other Jews. This sense of kinship finds sharpest public expression when Jews are in trouble. Jews find philanthropic and, more recently, political activity on behalf of other Jews more engaging than any other kind of Jewish activity—not only because it is what they do best or what they feel most comfortable doing, but because this activity is directed toward goals that American Jews consider of primary Jewish importance. They are far more likely to contribute money than to pray or read a Jewish book, because, in good measure, helping other Jews by contributing money comes closest to their notion of what Judaism is all about.

Both the Holocaust and the creation of Israel have intensified the American Jews' sense of kinship with other Jews by reminding them of the special condition and special interests of all Jews. The state of Israel does mean more to American Jews than helping other Jews in distress. But American Jewish support for Israel certainly does not stem from a sense of national affiliation or identity. Rather it increasingly represents the content of the Jewish religion. And for the most part, though less true today, it is religion that still provides the nominal façade and legitimation for the Jewish sense of peoplehood and its concomitant political, philanthropic, and organizational activities.

While it would be misleading to overestimate it, the American Jewish self-conception of Judaism as a religion does have some significance. It has many implications for Jewish organizational life that are beyond the purview of this study. With respect to the question of Jewish identity, it does mean that American Jews take "religion" per se seriously. The nonobservant American Jew is far more likely to seek personal and spiritual meaning in religion than is his Israeli counterpart. In fact, he is far more likely to view his own lack of religious observance with a sense of guilt than is the nonobservant Israeli. Furthermore, it is significant that activity on behalf of other Jews has led many young people to identify more closely with Judaism and to consider more seriously what meaning, if any, Judaism can have in their personal lives. In other words, when fund-raising and political activities are conducted on behalf of Jewish causes, they not only express deeply held social commitments but lead the activist to search for spiritual and personal meaning in Judaism. This experience is particularly true for many young leadership groups involved in fund raising for Israel and local Jewish needs.

The Intensity of Jewish Identity in America

How important a role does their Jewish identity play in the self-identity of American Jews? One might expect that since the typical American Jew can abandon his Jewish identity with relative ease, those who continue to identify themselves as Jews would be more self-consciously Jewish than the typical Israeli Jew. The fact that American Jews have gone through a process of self-selection, in which they had to wrestle with the choice of identity, would also seem to indicate that they sense their Jewish identity more intensely. This awareness, one might expect, would be reinforced by the minority status of the Jew, which should serve as a continual reminder of his Jewishness.

Although there is much truth in the foregoing, and it is applicable to many Jews, matters are not quite so simple. On the one hand, one is impressed by the number of young Jews whose Jewish identity is a central fact of their lives. But in the absence of reliable data the observer must ask himself if he really isn't more impressed by the existence of such youth rather than their absolute number. The number of American Jews who remain rather casual about their Jewishness runs into the millions. In the absence of antisemitism or an overtly Christian presence in public life, Jews can—without any sense of commitment—continue identifying with Jews out of familial loyalty, childhood associations, life-style preferences, or a sense of comfort in the presence of other Jews. Israel serves to remind them that Jewish life throughout the world is not always secure. The condition of Jews in other countries does not receive enough coverage in the American mass media to ensure a continued awareness of the problems of being Jewish in other parts of the world.

American Jews can be placed along a continuum of identity and participation in Jewish life. Daniel Elazar has suggested seven categories into which American Jews may be fitted.[7] He estimates that from 5 to 8 percent of American Jews (300,000–500,000 Jews) can be identified as Integral Jews—those whose Jewishness is a central concern of their lives, whether expressed in traditionally religious terms or through intensive involvement in Jewish affairs. For these Jews, "every day is lived by a substantially Jewish rhythm."[8] He calls the second category Participants and estimates their number at from 10 to 12 percent of the American Jewish population (600,000–700,000 Jews). The Participants take part in Jewish life in a regular way and are more than casually active in Jewish affairs, but their "rhythm of life is essentially that of the larger society."[9] Judaism to them is a major avocational interest.

Elazar calls the third category Associated Jews and estimates their number at roughly two million, or 30 to 35 percent of the American Jewish population. These are Jews who are affiliated with but not active in synagogues or mass membership organizations like Hadassah or B'nai B'rith. They use the synagogue for Jewish rites of passage or High Holy Day services but have no sustained interest in synagogue life. Their membership "reflects primarily private social interests rather than a concern for the public purposes of Jewish life."[10]

His fourth category, Contributors and Consumers, numbers 25 to 30 percent, or between 1.5 and 1.8 million Jews. They give money to Jewish causes from time to time and may periodically use the services of a synagogue for a wedding, a bar mitzvah, or a funeral. They regard themselves as Jews, but their communal association is minimal.

Some 15 percent, or roughly 900,000 Jews, fall into the category of Peripherals. They identify themselves as Jews but are totally uninvolved in Jewish life. Elazar also estimates that less than five percent of the Jewish community (roughly 200,000 Jews) are Repudiators—people who deny their Jewishness. This group has declined in number and is not as hostile as it once was to things Jewish. Finally, Elazar estimates that from five to ten percent of the total Jewish population are Quasi-Jews. These people, most of them married to non-Jews, are "assimilated to a point where the fact of their Jewish birth is incidental in every aspect."[11]

If one wishes to evaluate the intensity of the American Jews' identity, and particularly if one wishes to compare it with that of the Jewish identity of Israeli Jews, one must be clear about the definition of membership in the Jewish community. If we visualize a community of six million American Jews, the general estimate of the total number of American Jews, then it is clear that the majority are far more ignorant of and indifferent to Judaism than are the vast majority of Israelis. These are Jews by accident of birth. They would not benefit from denying their Jewish identity, nor do they pay for affirming it. But if we visualize the Jewish community as composed of those Jews who are affiliated with one or more Jewish organizations, we are in fact talking about those who have chosen to identify as Jews. Among them there is an intensity and seriousness of Jewish commitment that is quite remarkable because it has withstood the powerful assimilatory forces of American society and even shows signs of renewal.

The condition of American Orthodoxy, the loosely organized community of religiously observant Jews, sheds light on the intensity of Jewish identity in the community at large, even though the group comprises only a small minority of American Jews. The ability of the Orthodox to more or less stabilize the number of their adherents after a long period of attrition suggests that American environmental pressures need not necessarily destroy Jewish life. The move on the part of the Orthodox Jewish community toward more rigorous observance, which has characterized them in the last twenty years despite their growing affluence and secular education, suggests that, at least in some respects, Jewish institutions can overcome environmental pressures. Finally, the heightened role and status of Orthodox Jews within the American Jewish community reflects a recognition by the non-Orthodox that intense Jewish commitment is to be admired, not denigrated. This attitude is a relatively recent development. Until twenty or thirty years ago, American Jews, including those active and involved in Jewish life, were concerned that they not seem too parochial and provincial. Good Jewish parents worried about broadening their children's horizons at the expense of deepening their Jewish perspectives and experiences.

JEWISH IDENTITY IN ISRAEL AND AMERICA

We have observed that in both Israel and the United States Jewish self-conceptions contain a mix of religious and ethnic-national elements. But the mix is not the same, and even the labels don't mean the same thing to Jews in Israel and the United States. Israelis stress the national element of Jewishness. American Jews stress a religious self-conception with a more recent increase in ethnic feeling. The Israeli national definition implies obligations and responsibilities that American Jews do not accept. But whether the Israeli Jew conceives of his Judaism in primarily national terms or the American Jew in primarily religious or ethnic terms, all acknowledge that an obligation and responsibility for other Jews is a consequence of their identity.

Both sides agree that religion is an important component of Judaism. But the term "religion" means something different to each side. Religion to the Israeli Jew means Orthodox Judaism—strict observance of Jewish law. Observance of Jewish law is the base line by which the Israeli measures how "religious" one is. However, because the religious element is a less vital component in the Israeli's Jewish self-conception, he does not feel a sense of Jewish guilt in his not being religiously observant. American Jews have a more diffuse standard of religion. Religion means being a good person and living according to the ethical precepts of Judaism. Now this definition of a religious person conforms to American Protestant notions, and it is possible that Jews pay lip service to this concept without actually believing it. Furthermore, there is evidence that American Jews increasingly define proper religious behavior as at least a minimal observance of Jewish law. The pendulum has been swinging toward an affirmation of the importance of religious observance in the proper behavior of a Jew, but there still remains a vast difference between the Israeli and American Jewish definitions of what it means to be a religious Jew.

The chief differences between American and Israeli views of Judaism lie not so much in the definition of a religious Jew but in the concept of Judaism's role in one's life. In the United States, Judaism's ultimate test is found in the private domain. Although a feeling of kinship and peoplehood provides the major focus of Jewish identity, that feeling will atrophy if American Jews sense that Judaism has nothing to say to them at a personal level. The condition of Israel, or of Soviet Jewry, reminds American Jews of their kinship with others because American Jews *choose* to identify themselves as Jews. The current legitimacy of ethnic pluralism in the United States supports the assertion of a distinctive Jewish identity, but it would be a mistake to exaggerate the lasting significance of what is more than likely only a passing phase.

The sense of Jewish identity, internalized through familial, peer-group, and educational experiences depends, in the absence of perceived anti-semitism, on the Jew's feeling that he shares a universe of meaning with other Jews. In this respect, therefore, American Judaism is in competition with alternative meaning systems that might appeal to American Jews. It is in competition with professional associations and private nonsectarian groups, and is threatened by technological society, which denies the validity of any total meaning system. The future of American Judaism depends on its capacity to engage the individual Jew at the personal and private level. This is a function that no Jewish organization or institution except a distinctly religious one is able to perform.

In Israel, on the other hand, Judaism points to the public aspects of life. To phrase this somewhat differently—the test of Judaism in Israel is what it has to say to the civil aspects of the society.

It is conceivable that Israelis might conclude that Judaism has very little to say of political and social significance, but that it does provide a vehicle for personal expression, it does help one to confront problems of ultimate meaning, to deal with questions such as "who am I?" "what is my purpose in life?" "what is death?" "why do I suffer?" or to express the joy and wonderment of life or the awe of the ineffable. While this is conceivable, we find it unlikely. If Israeli Jews find that Judaism does not supply symbols that unite the society, does not provide legitimacy for the social order, and has nothing meaningful to say about the use of power or the purposes of the civil order, they are likely to turn away from a meaningful Jewish identity, and their personal spiritual quests will move in other directions. If these circumstances come to pass, it does not mean that Israeli Jews will no longer call themselves Jews. It does mean, especially in the event of peace in the area, that the Israeli's Jewishness will mean no more than the Anglicanism of the Englishman or the Protestantism of the American.

Many, perhaps most, Jewishly concerned Israelis see Judaism today as facing competition from alternate systems of social order and political values, not from alternate systems of personal meaning. This challenge does not mean that Judaism must necessarily oppose itself to alternate social and political systems, but it must at least show its contemporary relevance to them. This situation helps explain why religious and nonreligious Jews in Israel take religious political parties for granted. These parties exist not only to protect the interests of religious Jews but to assert their interpretation of the political meaning of the religious tradition. The latter function, as we suggest in the next chapter, is not the parties' primary one, but it has been strengthened in recent years.

– 2 –

Separation of Religion and State in Israel: A Program or a Slogan?

Since Judaism in Israel is defined by most Israelis as relevant to the public order and the political system, the question of separating religion and state must mean something other than it does in the West. The phrase "separation of religion and state" is frequently heard in debates over religious-state issues in Israel. But it is not always clear what proponents of separation mean by the term or what changes they foresee in Judaism's role in the state.

Separation of religion and state is only one alternative, extreme and rather uncommon, within the range of possible relations between religion and state. Among those countries where religion and state are deemed to be separate, there are differences in the actual role religion plays in the political and cultural life of the society. By the same token, the fact that there is no separation of religion and state in Israel does not tell us very much about the specific place of religion in the life of the state. We will discuss three levels at which, it seems to us, religion and state interact: the symbolic level, the institutional level, and the legislational level.

THE SYMBOLIC LEVEL

Symbols derived from the Jewish religious tradition are frequently invoked by leaders of Israel and adopted as symbols of the institutions of the state. The seven-branched candelabrum, for example, which is the official symbol of Israel, was chosen because of its important historical associations as a religious symbol. Israeli stamps frequently bear religious

---

The basic concepts in this essay were first developed in an article by the authors in Hebrew, which appeared in *Molad* (September 1972), pp. 71–89.

representations; biblical verses are invoked in speeches by political leaders, inscribed on banners in state parades and ceremonials, and engraved on public buildings. Virtually no one takes exception to this practice, although in the United States, Jews would be the first to protest similar usages as invasions of their religious freedom. The absence of such objections in Israel, even from those who ostensibly support separation, is best explained by the almost universal assent of Israeli Jews to the maintenance of Israel's Jewish identity; in other words, support for Israel as a Jewish state.

The founders of Israel chose Jewish representational symbols in order to emphasize the country's Jewish character. Since there is hardly any Jewish symbol that does not derive from a religious source, separation of religion and state, at least at the symbolic level, is impossible without rejecting the Jewish nature of the state.

The differences between Israel and the United States are instructive at this point. A fair generalization is that Americans have opposed any special relationship between their state and any of the ethnic-cultural groups that constitute its population. Separation is one means to assure that no such relationship develops. In a pluralist society such as the United States, the identification of the state with any one group would undermine the unity of the society and the loyalties of the various religious, racial, and ethnic groups to the larger political system. By contrast, Israel emphasizes its relationship to the Jews and Jewish culture because this is what unites the vast majority of the population and helps overcome other cultural-ethnic differences related to country of origin.

But what of the relations between Israel's non-Jewish citizens and their state? This problem is not the subject of our chapter, but two aspects of it shed light on our topic. The "religious question," as that term is used in Israel, always refers to relations between religious and non-religious Jews. Relations between Jews and Arabs, even within the borders of Israel and even when both parties are citizens of Israel, is referred to as a national question; Arabs are called "the minorities." Tensions between Arabs and Jews are ethnic or national-political tensions, not, except on rare occasions, religious tensions. On the other hand, since Jewish national identity is conditioned upon Jewish religious membership, members of other religions cannot enjoy the same status as Jews even if they are prepared to integrate themselves into the Jewish nation. Even among radical Jewish secularists, hardly anyone is ready to recognize a Muslim or Christian as a Jewish national.

This situation does not mean that the majority of Israelis favor defining Jewishness in accordance with *halakha* (religious law). But in 1958, when the government rejected the *halakha* as a criterion for registering an individual by nationality, it still conditioned registration as a national Jew on affiliation to the Jewish religion. Favoritism to Jews is not a consequence of nonseparation of religion and state. It stems from the inability to separate religion and nationality within Judaism. Hence, the very definition of Israel as a Jewish state means a preferred status for the Jewish religion.

The prominent role that the Jewish religion plays in the symbols of Israel and the inability to dissociate religion from nationalism is connected to the fact that large numbers of ostensibly secular Jews voluntarily partake in religious acts and ceremonies. Ritual circumcision, Bar-Mitzvah ceremonials, the absence of all private as well as public transportation on Yom Kippur, and even fasting on Yom Kippur are customs in which the vast majority of the Jewish population engage. As the proportion of the more traditional Sephardic Jews increases and the proportion of Ashkenazic Jews declines, this trend can be expected to intensify. Israeli holidays, except for Independence Day, are essentially religious holidays, even if the majority of the population does not celebrate them in accordance with traditional law. But the fact that the vast majority of nonreligious Jews are willing to integrate elements of the Jewish tradition into their personal lives and, therefore, find their incorporation into the symbol system of the state unexceptionable, does not mean that they attribute the same meaning to those symbols as do religious Jews. Many impose a national rather than a peculiarly religious meaning upon the symbols. There has been opposition in secular circles to symbolic verbal expressions of a decidedly religious nature upon which it was difficult to impose national or social meaning. The most significant example was the controversy over the inclusion of the word "God" in Israel's Declaration of Independence. The eventual compromise, the term "rock of Israel," is typical of resolutions to controversies at the symbolic level: the different sides arrive at a symbol that each group can interpret in accordance with its proclivities. Among the religious, the term refers to God; the nonreligious could interpret it as referring to the Jewish people. On the other hand, the very example we cite, deriving from the period preceding the establishment of the state, when secularism existed as an ideology as well as a style of life, hints at the changes that have taken place since then. The decline of secular ideology, not unrelated to the rising demographic and political importance of the Sephardic population, facilitated the penetration of religious symbols into Israeli culture with greater frequency and intensity. Menachem Begin is the first Israeli prime minister to invoke the name of God regularly in his speeches, and it has probably helped his popularity. It remains to be seen how his successor will behave.

Most nonreligious Jews today do have a positive orientation to the Jewish tradition; they simply draw the line at observing the religious commandments. Political and educational leaders, long before the incumbency of Begin as prime minister or National Religious Party representative Zevulun Hammer as Minister of Education, sought to inculcate a positive attitude toward religion among Israeli youth. Such efforts began in the 1950s with the adoption by a labor-dominated government of the Jewish Consciousness program in Israeli schools. This effort reflected the failure of the political and cultural elite to find a secular Jewish foundation for Israeli national identity.

Not all symbolic questions have been resolved. The best example is the "Who is a Jew?" question; that is, can one be defined as Jewish by nationality if one isn't Jewish by religion? And how does one define a Jew by religion? The sharp controversy over an issue that is virtually devoid of practical consequences testifies to the continued importance of symbols in questions of religion and state. The support that many nonreligious Jews offered to the religious camp on this issue further indicates that many Jews in Israel who are not punctilious in religious observance recognize the association between religion and nationality in Judaism and are unwilling to support a conception of Jewish nationality in which a religious component is absent.

Of course, an association between religion and state at the symbolic level does not mean that they cannot be separated at the institutional or legislative level. Although it is impossible to fully compartmentalize these levels, since there is a symbolic significance to relationships between religion and state at the institutional or legislative level, there are states such as England, Sweden, or Denmark where nonseparation is almost purely symbolic. Such is not the case in Israel.

THE INSTITUTIONAL LEVEL

There are a number of different types of religious institutions accorded governmental status and funded by the state. They include the chief rabbis and Chief Rabbinical Council, local chief rabbis, local religious councils, and rabbinical courts. In addition the Ministry of Religious Affairs and

Ministry of the Interior fund a variety of religious institutions and services, and the Ministry of Education and Culture provides for a state religious school system parallel to the state nonreligious school system. As we indicated, the governmental status of religious institutions is of symbolic significance, particularly in religious Zionist circles. They perceive this status as confirmation of the Jewish-religious character of Israel. Furthermore, because the state is viewed as possessing special sanctity, governmental-religious institutions have that much greater importance. But the political institutionalization of religion has significance and meaning beyond the symbolic level because such status confers a measure of legal authority and establishes eligibility for public funding.

Non-Jewish religious institutions also benefit from state support. But Israelis are generally indifferent to these institutions and do not think of them as part of the controversy over religious-state relations in Israel. Muslim and Christian religious courts are recognized by the state and possess exclusive judicial authority in matters of the personal status (marriage and divorce) of their adherents. Muslim and Druze institutions and religious services are recognized and funded by the state. Christian groups declined government assistance in order to safeguard their autonomy. In fact, religious discrimination in Israel is not directed against non-Jewish religions but against non-Orthodox Jewish religious groups.[1]

The institutional monopoly of the Orthodox (Conservative and Reform rabbis are not recognized as rabbis in Israel, and Conservative and Reform synagogues are discriminated against in distribution of state support, though they do receive some benefits) is not a major political issue. There are no more than two or three thousand members of non-Orthodox synagogues, and, as we shall see in other instances, issues of religious conscience do not arouse Israelis. Finally, not unrelated to this last point, while only about 20 percent of the Jewish population are observant Jews, many others, Sephardim in particular, accept Orthodox assumptions about what the Jewish religion is all about.

The central issue in religious-state relations at the institutional level has been the degree of autonomy to be granted to religious institutions— the extent of the state's right to supervise the activity and influence the structure and policy of these institutions. This is the issue that lies at the heart of the controversies over the election of the chief rabbis, the appointment of local rabbinical councils, the status and organization of the state-religious educational system, or, to cite the most recent issue, the funding of religious institutions by the Ministry of the Interior through local governments whose officials know nothing about them.

The most important public services in the field of religion (except for education) are provided by local religious councils. They support local synagogues and subsidize rabbis' salaries, they are responsible for supervision of dietary laws in commercial establishments and for maintaining local ritualariums, and they will often sponsor or assist in local adult-educational programs. These semi-autonomous groups are funded by the central and local government. But they are composed of religious or at least traditional Jews, most of whom are members of the National Religious Party (NRP). Secularists protest that this set-up means giving a minority of the population authority over state institutions and the use of public funds. Their demand, however, is not to degovernmentalize the services the councils perform but to make them truly representative bodies or to transfer the overseeing of religious services to bodies representing the general public, such as local governments. Religious circles, on the other hand, object to any supervision by secularists or to their membership on the religious councils. The more extreme religious Jews in particular are also dissatisfied with the current composition of the religious councils. Despite the fact that members must swear that they bear a positive attitude toward the tradition, and most are NRP members, some are *de facto* representatives of secular parties and sit on the religious councils to do their party's bidding. In addition, the authority of the local government to approve the religious council budget affords it a degree of supervision and limits the council's autonomy.

A similar controversy surrounds the status of other religious institutions, such as the chief rabbinate and rabbinical courts. Secular circles strive to increase state influence on the composition and policies of the religious institutions, and religious circles struggle to defend the autonomy of the institutions. The outcome is not entirely satisfactory to anybody. Major influence remains with the religious sector, whose representatives constitute a majority of the electoral body that selects the chief rabbis and judges of the rabbinical courts. But nonreligious representatives are not bereft of influence. This is an appropriate point to observe that despite the legal recognition accorded to religious institutions, they are not fully and organically integrated into the governmental system. A large proportion of Israel's population, including many political and judicial bodies, refuse to recognize the rabbinate's status except in those specific, rather narrow, areas where legislation has conferred authority upon them. On the other hand, the rabbinate insists *de jure* on its own autonomy in relation to the state; it denies that the judicial system or, for that matter, the Knesset has the moral right to impose its authority upon it. Whereas the Supreme Court of Israel insists that rabbinical courts derive their authority from Knesset law, and therefore must accept the rule of that law and the authority of the secular courts, the religious institutions claim that their authority derives from *halakha,* and it is *halakha* alone to which they are subservient. In other words, despite the formal pattern of relations between institutions of religion and those of the state, the two systems exist somewhat independently with each believing that its authority is derived from and legitimated by a different source. However, except for rabbinical courts that possess legal authority to adjudicate matters of personal status, the remaining religious institutions have no real authority to compel obedience in matters of consequence to the nonreligious public. Hence, the public can afford relative indifference to their existence, even to their continued receipt of public money, which represents, after all, an inconsequential part of the total government budget. We are inclined to believe, however, that public support for conferring governmental status on religious institutions stems from a positive attitude toward the existence of such institutions rather than from indifference to their policies.

It is clear from this discussion that the controversy over religious-state relations at the institutional level is not over the principle of separation. Virtually every political party in Israel supports the funding of religious institutions despite evidence of misuse of funds and even corruption. In the United States, the principle of religious-state separation means prohibition of direct state support for religious services. In Israel, on the other hand, provision of religious services is assumed to be a function of government. This function extends to what the religious public considers to be the most important of all religious institutions: religious schools.

Religious education is the central issue of the religious-state conflict in many nations. Controversy surrounded the issue in Israel as well and occasioned the fall of one government and crises in others. But in most countries the issue is whether the state is to recognize and support religious schools. In the United States and other countries where separation is the rule, nonsupport for religious education is one of the foundation stones of the separation principle. In Israel, hardly anyone questions the principle of state support for religious schools. In fact, even the curriculum of the nonreligious state schools in Israel violates the principles of separation because of the time devoted to specifically religious studies. The controversy in Israel centers on the question of the status and organization of religious education in comparison to the nonreligious educational system. The principal question is whether the religious sector alone or the state is to direct and supervise the religious education in state-religious schools, which enroll about 25 percent of elementary-school-age children. The state has long conceded the *de facto* right of Agudat Israel (also referred to as Agudah), the non-Zionist religious party, to operate an independent religious school system, which attracts under 10 percent of the elementary-school-age population and which the state funds.

Every state supports activity that concerns only one subgroup or another within the population. But we can distinguish between states according to whether or not the general society supervises the services of the different subgroups and determines what services are to be provided. We can conceive of two radically different possibilities. One possibility is that society, through its governmental representatives, determines that a particular activity or service deserves public support even if only one sector of the population will benefit. The society, in turn, reserves full authority to direct these services in accordance with the national interest. To push the case to its extreme, the population subgroup to receive the services would be based not on birth (race or ethnicity) or on ideology (religion or political preference) but on categories into which any member of the population might, under certain circumstances, fall (e.g., age, income, health). An example of this form of service would be welfare assistance, or care for the aged. The government decides that it is in its interest to assist one segment of the population, and it does so in the form of aid that it administers. But there is an alternative possibility for providing governmental service, which we can label institutionalized pluralism. In this system, the government subsidizes one or another subgroup that is either communally or institutionally organized, and the group itself decides how and to whom the money is to be distributed. In the ideal-typical case the subgroups would not necessarily be those into which every member of the population might fall. An example is public support for black community schools in New York City in the 1960s. Local community councils, all of whom were black, were given control over the schools in their neighborhoods.

In reality, no society functions purely on the basis of this extreme example of pluralism. But we can compare the degree to which the national-interest principle prevails over the group-autonomy (or institutionalized-pluralism) principle in different societies. The variations between societies probably stem from historical and cultural traditions and technological development. We may assume that in a culturally homogeneous, technologically advanced society, whose political leaders see themselves as administrators and executors, not group representatives, services will be provided by the government in terms of the national interest. Such a state will also provide services to subsectors of the populations, but they will be perceived as national services that happen to be required by only one section of the society—not as a subsidy to one particular group within the society.

In Jewish society in Palestine in the period of the British mandate, and for that matter during the first years of statehood, the prevailing social-political culture legitimated the group-autonomy or institutionalized-pluralism principle. Ben Gurion devoted much energy to combatting this principle, which was steadily eroded after 1948. Its presence, however, is still felt. The Israeli public is far more inclined than the English public, for example, to fund activities and services that are exclusively directed to a subgroup of the population out of consideration for the status of that group rather than out of consideration for the type of service provided. The reasons stem from the absence of a strong central authority in the prestate period and from the political traditions of Eastern European and Muslim societies, where the vast majority of the population originated. On the other hand, the notion of subgroup autonomy is increasingly falling out of favor in Israel. The benefits and autonomy that the Histadrut (the General Federation of Labor) or the kibbutzim enjoyed in the past, for example, began to lose their legitimacy in the public mind years before the rise to power of the Likud, which sought to restrict these benefits for its own political reasons. In many respects, the privileges and autonomy enjoyed by the religious sector are the last major stronghold of the institutionalized-pluralism principle.

The autonomy of religious institutions is strengthened by the zealousness with which the religious public defends them and the vehemence with which it opposes any effort by the state to interfere in religious matters. The corollary of nonseparation of religion and state has traditionally been some state control of religious institutions and some voice in the formation of religious policy. The religious public is vigilant in opposing such efforts despite the fact that they are a natural outcome of nonseparation. Withdrawing state support for religious institutions and services is not even an issue in Israel. The real issue is state supervision, which the religious public has been relatively successful in avoiding.

In conclusion, at both the institutional and symbolic levels, there is hardly any support for separation of religion and state. The vast majority of the public is satisfied with religious-state relations or has never seriously considered an alternative arrangement. This acceptance is not the case, however, at the third level of religious-state involvement.

Religious Legislation

By religious legislation we mean those laws or administrative regulations that compel citizens to obey religious commandments. For example, the exclusive jurisdiction conferred upon rabbinical courts in matters of the personal status of Jews is an obvious imposition of *halakha*, even if the immediate authority for that imposition is the Knesset itself rather than the rabbis. The laws that arouse the greatest antagonism and controversy among the nonreligious are Sabbath rest laws.

The Sabbath and Jewish holidays are official days of rest. Most industrial and commercial activity is prohibited by the statute regulating hours of work and rest and not by a "Sabbath Law," which has often been proposed but never legislated. Most public controversy, however, surrounds national legislation and local ordinances prohibiting in almost every city the operation of local transportation, restaurants, and places of entertainment on the Sabbath.

Not all the nonreligious public objects to these laws. Nonreligious Sephardic Jews are more sympathetic than nonreligious Ashkenazic Jews. But the laws do evoke widespread dissatisfaction. We believe that this dissatisfaction stems from the personal discomfort or inconvenience that these laws cause rather than from an objection to religious coercion. This distinction explains why nonobservant Jews who are opposed to certain kinds of religious legislation can accept religious legislation of a purely symbolic or institutional nature, or even laws that coerce religious conscience.

One expects that a stance that bases itself on freedom of conscience will be uncompromising, absolute, and indifferent to the rules of the political game or the balance of political forces in the society. Those who oppose religious legislation on grounds of conscience believe that such legislation violates the principles of democracy, even if it is supported by a majority of the public; for it is a basic principle of democracy that even a majority cannot compel the minority to act in violation of its religious beliefs. But not all religious legislation, even when it is of a compelling character, violates religious conscience. In our opinion, the only religious legislation in Israel that involves the violation of religious conscience is the marriage-and-divorce law.

Laws concerning Sabbath rest or prohibitions on pig raising coerce the public, but it is far-fetched to believe that they violate anyone's religious belief. It is, therefore, of great significance in understanding religious-state issues that whereas large segments—probably a majority—of the nonreligious population are reconciled to religious coercion or violations of conscience in matters of marriage and divorce, there is widespread opposition to Sabbath closing laws—matters of convenience but not conscience. The rabbinical courts have in fact lost none of their power over marriage and divorce, but more and more industrial and commercial establishments are permitted to remain open on the Sabbath.

There are some who are upset that marriage and divorce of Jews in Israel must be conducted in accordance with religious law. But an important distinction can be made in what that public finds offensive. Let us take the marriage law, for example. First of all, Jewish partners, in order to be married, have to undergo Orthodox procedures, some of which may be offensive and demeaning to nonreligious Jews. Second, *halakha* prohibits the marriage of certain partners whom Western law permits to be married. For example, a male *kohen* (someone descended from Aaron, the first high priest) cannot marry a divorcee; a *mamzer* (someone born of an illicit, e.g., an adulterous, union) can only marry another *mamzer* or a convert to Judaism. Significantly, it is this second aspect of the law to which opponents take strongest exception. Demands to permit such marriages generally arise when a particularly outrageous incident catches the public's attention. Pressure is then exerted to find some solution to the particular problem. Former Chief Rabbi Goren, in his first few years in office, was often most helpful in finding a resolution to such problems. As soon as a solution is found, or with the passage of time if none is found, public clamor subsides. Proposals offered in the Knesset to correct these abuses generally provide for the possibility of civil marriage where rabbinical as distinct from Western law prohibits the parties from marrying. The proposals, except where offered by representatives of fringe parties, do not provide for a marriage at which a Reform or Conservative rather than an Orthodox rabbi officiates, or for a civil marriage between two Jewish partners who find a religious ceremony repugnant to their convictions. In fact, one of the arguments that those who defend the status quo feel is most convincing is that if any form of civil marriage is permitted, Israel will find it awkward to prohibit marriages between Jews and non-Jews. Former prime minister Golda Meir herself offered this as an argument in the Knesset. Hardly anyone is troubled by the *de facto* prohibition of interreligious marriage.

From a religious point of view there is a measure of self-sacrifice in many of the demands for religious legislation. Religious Jews don't require these laws for themselves. They don't need Sabbath rest laws or prohibitions on raising pigs or religious marriage-and-divorce laws in order to live their lives in accordance with *halakha*. The coercion that they seek to impose on the nonreligious threatens their relations with them, invites retaliation, and, as many realize, is counterproductive in bringing the nonreligious to a greater appreciation of the religious tradition. To the extent that religious parties seek coercive legislation, they do so primarily out of a sense of religious responsibility for nonreligious Jews and because their commitment to the state (not to religion) depends to some extent on the Jewish-religious character of the state.

The religious parties choose to rationalize their demands for religious legislation in secular terms. Arguments they offer include the importance of preserving national unity (civil marriage and divorce, they argue, would split the country and create a category of Jews whom religious Jews could not marry), or the desire not to alienate Diaspora Jewry (at least until recently Diaspora Jewry was assumed to be more Orthodox than the majority of Israelis), or the moral-social significance of the law (Sabbath rest laws were rationalized on a social welfare basis), or even the security of Israel (non-Orthodox conversion to Judaism is condemned as too easy, facilitating infiltration of hostile elements). This form of rationalization is best explained by its propagandistic value. While those who offer these arguments probably believe them, we do not believe that they provide the impetus for religious legislation. The impetus stems in good part from an authentic national-religious impulse, however unfortunate the nonreligious may find its consequences to be.

There is a second impetus for religious legislation that, at least until the last few years, played a more important role and distinguished between issues that aroused the religious public to a pitch and the kind of issues to which they responded with relative passivity. The major goal of the religious public was the protection of their own interests and rights as a distinctive sector within the general population. It is true that, in general, Agudat Israel tended to be more concerned with protecting its own constituency and the NRP relatively more concerned with imposing a Judaic character and a climate of religious observance on the general population. But even the NRP was primarily concerned with the interests of the religious public. The core commitment to religious parties stems from their supporters' belief that the parties will defend them as a group and as individuals. One of their basic concerns is protecting yeshiva students and religious girls from involuntary military service. (A yeshiva [plural: yeshivot] is a school for advanced talmudic study. The issue of military service is more important to Agudah than to the NRP.) Other objectives of the religious parties are that religious institutions retain their autonomy, that autopsies not be performed on religious Jews against their wishes, and that the religious parties act as mediators in governmental provision of services and benefits to religious settlements, religious economic enterprises, and religious schools from nursery to university. Religious voters are far less committed to imposing a general Sabbath law or banning television on the Sabbath.

It would appear that in recent years, religious voters have become more concerned with issues affecting all Israelis than with protecting their own interests as a special sector. This change stems, in good measure, from the fact that religious voters feel increasingly more secure that their basic interests are protected. This development in turn stems from a number of factors, not the least important of which is the Likud's rise to power and Begin's premiership. The sense of security of religious voters is also related to the weakening of secular ideology and antireligious sentiment in Israel and the growing penetration of religious symbols into Israeli culture. Finally, it stems from the presence of Israeli-born religious Jews who are more at home in Israeli culture, less isolated and alienated from nonreligious Israelis, and less anxious about defending their group or engaging in activities of a general social nature than were the NRP's founders. These changes have persuaded former NRP voters that the defense of religious interests no longer requires the same vigilance. It permits them the luxury of supporting nonreligious parties. But the NRP itself has felt freer to engage in broader political issues—foreign policy in particular. Even Agudat Israel, heretofore concerned almost exclusively with protection of its constituents' interests, has sought the passage of religious legislation of a general nature (e.g., amending the "Who is a Jew?" law or imposing more stringent Sabbath observance or anti-abortion laws on the population at large).

It is our belief that the defense of narrow religious interests still lies closest to the hearts of religious voters and that basic changes in this regard have not taken place. Contrary to popular opinion, the fiercest conflicts over religious issues have broken out not in response to attempted religious coercion but in response to what the religious public interpreted as antireligious coercion—that is, interference by secular circles in religious matters and in the right of religious Jews to conduct their lives in accordance with their principles. Furthermore, the effort to impose religious legislation arouses the bitterest antagonism of the secular public, and this realization also influences the religious public to content itself with the status quo. For their part, most nonreligious groups, at least most of their political representatives, are reluctant to undermine their partnership with the religious groups and are therefore unwilling to challenge the status quo in the field of religious legislation. In addition there is a large, predominantly Sephardic sector of the public that is happy with the present arrangement, particularly in the areas of Sabbath observance and marriage and divorce. This satisfaction stems from their positive orientation to various facets of the tradition and their desire to enhance the Jewish nature of Israel by integrating aspects of the tradition into the legal code.

These various orientations help explain the relatively moderate nature of the controversy over religious legislation despite sharp differences of opinion and basic values.

Integration or Separation of Religion and State

Religion and state are associated with each other at various levels in Israel, but the association is by no means complete. Indeed, the very existence of a religious sector as a distinctive cultural subgroup within the population prevents the organic integration of religion into the national elements of the political culture, particularly when this subgroup strives so vigorously to maintain the autonomy and independence of its religious institutions. There are some secularists who protest that the obstinacy of the religious sector in preserving its distinctive values prevents a more complete incorporation of elements from the tradition into the general educational system and culture. The complaint is made that Orthodox Jews assume a monopoly on the values of the tradition and on religious education and hinder the non-Orthodox from identifying with these values. Members of the religious sector, it is charged, are anxious to influence society at large but unwilling to adapt the laws and values of the tradition in order to anchor them in contemporary culture. There is, in fact, an underlying tension between those secularists, even of the ultranationalist political right, who welcome the integration of the values and symbols of the tradition into Israeli culture and the political and spiritual leaders of the religious public who are often aligned politically with the ultranationalists but are wary of their exploitation of the tradition.

The Orthodox problem is that unless they are prepared to compromise *halakhic* principles, they have no hope for imposing their own Jewish conceptions on Israel, that is, for conducting the state in accordance with *halakha.* Separation of religion and state, on the other hand, relieves them of pressure to compromise the *halakha* but divorces Israel of Jewish meaning as far as they understand it and makes it difficult for them to identify with the state. The problem is especially acute for religious Zionists, who attribute sanctity to the existence of Israel, which they view as the beginning of divine redemption. For that very reason they sense with special poignancy the gap between the ideal state as they envision it and the real Israel. But separation of religion and state is the alternative they are least likely to embrace.

The secularists' problem is no easier. The vast majority of them desire to maintain the national unity of Jews and the historical continuity of the Jewish nation. They want to impart content to their own Jewish identity and that of Israel. But they are not Orthodox Jews; they are unwilling to observe religious law and do not subscribe to the dogmas of Jewish faith. They are certainly unwilling to permit the *halakha* to rule over public life. This attitude means finding an alternative mode of Jewish identity, and this search has, so far, proven unrewarding.

The result is the present condition: neither separation of religion and state nor total integration. It is a complex situation in which no side is entirely satisfied. But it is difficult to suggest an alternative. Furthermore, complete separation would not resolve all religious conflicts: for example, the drafting of religious girls or declarations by rabbinical authorities recommending that religious Jews not fly El Al or travel by Israeli ship. These and other controversies have no relationship to separation or nonseparation or to the Orthodox monopoly over the interpretation of religious law in Israel.

The present condition reflects the effort to overcome, by political agreement, problems that stem from cultural-religious differences concerning the ideal structure and direction of Israeli society. These agreements do not resolve the basic problem, and no political arrangement is likely to do so. What the agreements do is facilitate the coexistence and cooperation of the religious and nonreligious sectors. These arrangements depend on the consensus that Israel must remain a Jewish state and that ways have to be found to maintain the unity of the Jewish population. This consensus overlays deep divisions of opinion concerning the definition of Jewish life and the nature of Israel implicit in its definition as a Jewish state. Recognition of this division, in turn, leads to the systematic effort to refrain from principled decisions requiring one side or another to surrender its vision or conception of the meaning of a Jewish state. This, more than any other reason, explains why both sides continue to appeal to the status quo in state-religious arrangements as the basic criterion by which issues are to be resolved.

One frequently hears criticism within Israel of political horse-trading on religious issues: concessions by one side, usually the religious, in return for political appointments or funding of religious institutions. Within the religious public there is a sense that their political representatives often sell out for narrow political advantage, and this behavior seems particularly reprehensible in matters of religion, which are presumably matters of ultimate principle. We hold no particular brief for the leaders of Israel's religious parties. As a group they are as unsavory as the political leaders of any other party. But what is often forgotten is that the existential and fundamental basis of the conflict over religion and state on the one hand and the desire to maintain national unity on the other also leads to a conciliatory political style based on mutual concession and abjuration of total victory.

– 3 –

The "Status Quo" Agreement as a Solution to Problems of Religion and State in Israel

The basis for conflict resolution of religion-state issues rests, as we indicated in the last chapter, on agreement among the opposing parties about the need to maintain national unity and preserve the Jewish character of the state. This agreement is embedded in an ostensibly operative document known as the "Status Quo."

At the first sign of public controversy between religious and secular political forces in Israel, the aggrieved party (sometimes both parties) appeals to the status quo, maintaining that the other side is violating its provisions. The status quo has an almost sanctified aura to it. It functions in many cases like a constitution that no one fully understands and that lends itself to multiple interpretations, but it plays an important mythic role in projecting a belief that there are firm criteria and a fixed process for resolving political disputes and that maintenance of the process is more important than the advantage to be gained by one side or another in a particular controversy.

The history of the status quo agreement in religious affairs is really a history of the development of relations between religion and state in Israel. The interpretation of the status quo was a source of controversy between religious and nonreligious Jews, but was also the basis for the resolution of these controversies. It was during the period of the *yishuv* (the modern prestate Jewish settlement in Palestine) that the main elements constituting the agreement were crystallized.

This chapter is based on an article in Hebrew by Eliezer Don-Yehiya, "The Status-Quo Solution in the Area of Religion and State," *Medina V'memshal,* no. 6 (1971): 100–12.

The Background to the Status Quo Agreement

In June 1947 the Executive Committee of Agudat Israel, the non-Zionist religious party, received a letter from the chairman of the Jewish Agency, David Ben Gurion, the political leader of the *yishuv*, offering a number of promises with respect to public control of religious matters in the soon-to-be established state. The letter promised that: (1) Saturday would be set aside as the national day of rest; (2) dietary laws (*Kashrut*) would be observed in all kitchens under government auspices; (3) religious courts would maintain exclusive jurisdiction over marriage and divorce laws; and (4) the existing autonomous religious educational systems would be recognized by the future state.

These four promises assured the leadership of Agudat Israel that the principal arrangements regarding religious-state relations that prevailed before 1948 would be maintained in the future; hence the term "status quo."[1] Let us trace the basic elements of the status quo agreement in the order of their development.

The question of education was the basis for the establishment of Mizraḥi (the religious Zionist movement) in 1902. Mizraḥi's primary goal was to oppose the demand that the Zionist movement engage in cultural activities aimed at developing and disseminating "national culture." Religious Zionists feared that whereas such a culture might adopt many symbols of the tradition, it would be basically secular rather than religious and would offer a new form of Jewish self-definition. Mizraḥi did not insist that the Zionist movement accept a religious definition of Jewish nationalism, i.e., that its source was the Torah or God. But they resisted the attempt to equate Zionism with a secular concept of a Jewish "national culture."

Mizraḥi advocated cooperative efforts between religious and nonreligious Zionists in securing the political goals of the movement and in practical work on behalf of settlements in the land of Israel. But it insisted that both sides refrain from advocating positions on matters of religion and culture, issues that were not to concern the Zionist movement. In other words, according to Mizraḥi, education and cultural activity were to lie outside the purview of Zionism.

This proposal elicited support among many nonreligious Zionists, Herzl and his followers in particular. They, the political Zionists, had a single-minded preoccupation with securing the political basis for the establishment of a Jewish homeland and were indifferent to or feared the divisive effect of other issues.[2]

Those who favored expanding the scope of Zionist activity to cultural affairs gradually won the upper hand within the World Zionist Organization, of which Mizraḥi was a member. This development led some Mizraḥi members to secede and establish Agudat Yisrael in 1912. Those who remained in Mizraḥi now insisted that since the Zionist movement was to undertake educational activity, including establishing or supporting existing schools in the land of Israel, Mizraḥi should be commissioned to direct an autonomous religious educational system. The demand was presented as a condition for their remaining within the movement, and it was accepted. In 1920, two separate educational systems were established for the *yishuv*, a religious and a general one. It was this ideological and organizational principle that the status quo agreement confirmed, in addition to Agudat Israel's right to maintain its own independent school system.

Another element of the status quo agreement addresses itself indirectly to the principle of religious autonomy. Under Ottoman rule, the Jewish community, like other minorities, was permitted its own religious judicial system, which was recognized by the state. When the British acquired Palestine under the League of Nations mandate following World War I, they adopted the Ottoman system as a means for maintaining political peace.

Observance of the Sabbath by public institutions is a third element in the status quo agreement. The Second Zionist Congress in 1898 resolved that "Zionism will not act in any way to infringe upon the Jewish religion." The religious Zionists inferred from this that no official activities of the Zionist movement would take place on the Sabbath. The nonreligious interpreted it otherwise, and bitter disputes within the movement erupted, particularly following the expansion of Zionist activities in the land of Israel under the British mandate.

At the Nineteenth Zionist Congress, held in 1935, a settlement was reached between Mizraḥi and Mapai, the dominant Zionist party. According to the agreement, no public desecration of the Sabbath was to occur, and dietary laws were to be maintained in public institutions.

From 1935 on, there was *de facto* recognition of the status quo principles as the basis for cooperation between religious and nonreligious Jews, first in the *yishuv* and later in the state of Israel. The principles also served as a point of departure for the resolution of religious questions that might arise in the future. The Ben Gurion letter, therefore, confirmed what leadership on both sides had come to accept.

Moderate elements among both religious and nonreligious groups sought to continue their working partnership. The status quo is a convenient and pragmatic solution to religious questions in Israel for moderate elements, since it requires neither side to abandon any of its principles.

The term "status quo" is something of a misnomer, since changes of considerable significance have taken place in the relationship between the two sides. But more often than not, the two sides have chosen to ignore these changes, or they have permitted them to become regularized and then pretended that they were always present. The political principle underlying the status quo is that each side refrains from declaring its intention to introduce any changes. In this way, no decisions that could be interpreted as a surrender or concession of principles are ever undertaken.[3] It also means that many changes evolve gradually rather than being initiated by Knesset legislation. But because the process remains informal, the door is open to changes of minor and sometimes major details, depending on the current social climate or constellation of political forces. The status quo, therefore, is a useful, though by no means perfect, instrument for resolving conflicts over religion and state.

Following the establishment of the state of Israel, leaders on both sides believed that the status quo was the most suitable instrument for regulating questions about the status of religion in the new state. Even those who were unhappy with the particulars of the agreement did not demand its overthrow. Instead, they pointed to the continued expansion of areas under the control of the religious parties and sought to restore the balance. In later years, it was the religious side that generally felt aggrieved. Since 1977 and the Likud victory, the pendulum has again swung in the opposite direction.

To some, however, the changes that took place following the establishment of the state of Israel and the mass immigration meant that the status quo was incapable of constituting an effective basis for the prevention or resolution of conflicts between religious and nonreligious. This assessment was particularly true in the cases to be described below. As we shall see, however, the specifics of the status quo may have been inadequate, but the framework survived intact.

The Education Crisis

The existence of two autonomous educational systems could flourish only in a relatively stable society. After the establishment of the state of Israel and the mass immigration of Jews that followed, competition between the two systems erupted. Because the existing educational network was not equipped to absorb the large number of children who lived mainly in *maabarot* (transit camps built for immigrants), special schools were established for them. The parents of the children were unfamiliar with the ideological differences between the two educational systems. The subsequent competition for the immigrant children led to sharp tensions. To reduce the tension, the government decided that instead of incorporating the immigrant childrens' schools into the existing dual-system network, the schools in the *maabarot* would function under the supervision of the cultural branch of the Ministry of Education. Religious lessons were to be offered to those interested. Representatives of the religious parties opposed this solution. Recriminations and physical disturbances broke out in the *maabarot* and stormy discussions took place in the Knesset. It was then decided that immigrant children from Yemen (all of whose parents were religious) would receive religious education. Immigrants from the remaining countries would have the option of choosing between religious and nonreligious education. But Mapai was unwilling to concede authority over the religious schools to Mizrahi, lest the schools become instruments for socializing the masses of newly arrived youngsters to religious parties.

In prestate Israel, Mapai did not deal with religious education. Since the number of religious immigrants in those days was small, it was the religious parties who saw to the education of the religious population. Following the establishment of the state of Israel, Mapai, like all other parties, sought to enlist the support of the masses of new immigrants. Since so many immigrants were religious, Mapai established a new school system committed to "traditional values" as well as "labor values." The status quo, therefore, appeared ineffective in preventing or resolving conflict under the radically changed circumstances.

Since it was not possible to reach a new agreement, or to keep the existing one, a governmental crisis broke out and new elections were held. When the elections showed virtually no shift in the balance of power, both sides realized that they had to resolve their differences, and a new law regulating education in Israel was passed. The state-controlled school systems were now established—one secular and one religious. The new law permitted Ben Gurion to achieve his goal of centralizing all secular schools under state control, and, in return for support on this issue, Mizrahi was, in fact, after some further dispute, granted practical though not theoretical control over state religious schools. Agudat Israel was permitted to operate its own small independent school system, which was given even greater autonomy than that enjoyed by Mizrahi schools.

Following passage of the law in 1953, the controversy abated. Conflicts did not cease completely, but compared to the agitation during the preceding years, the situation was well under control.

In summary, the status quo was undermined in the area of education in the years following the establishment of the state of Israel as a result of the influx of immigrants. Stability was later reestablished. The system of autonomous educational systems was abolished, yet no fundamental change really took place.

The Status of the Religious Institutions and the Composition of the Chief Rabbinate and the Religious Councils

There are differences in the nature and authority of the various Jewish religious institutions in Israel. The major institutions are:

1. Religious councils: These councils are administrative bodies in each locality that provide religious services such as supervising the slaughter of meat, maintaining religious food laws in public institutions, paying local religious officials, and supporting synagogues.
2. The chief rabbis and rabbinical council: The two chief rabbis, one Sephardic and one Ashkenazic, assisted by a number of advisors, constitute the Chief Rabbinical Council. The formal authority of the chief rabbis and the council is limited, but most religious Zionists accept their decisions as binding.
3. Local chief rabbis: Generally two rabbis, one Sephardic and one Ashkenazic, serve as spiritual leaders to the local religious population. Like the chief rabbis, they possess no binding legal powers but a great deal of prestige among local religious Zionists. Sephardic Jews, even when they are not religious, are especially deferential toward their rabbis.
4. The rabbinical courts: They possess exclusive and binding authority over the entire population in matters under their jurisdiction. For this reason, as we will shortly see, it was not possible to leave the rabbinical courts in an undefined legal state, as were the Chief Rabbinical Council and the religious councils.

Religious institutions in the period of the Mandate possessed governmental authority but were independent of the political institutions of the

The "Status Quo" Agreement as a Solution

yishuv. Such a condition was difficult for an independent state to accept. On the other hand, new legislative initiatives would have met with serious controversy among the public and would have required a new set of arrangements between religious and secular leaders. For this reason, it was decided that the arrangement in effect during the time of the Mandate would serve as the basis for determining the scope of authority and election procedures for the Chief Rabbinical Council and the local religious councils. The manner in which this issue was handled illustrates the principles behind the status quo: avoiding changes that would upset either party, avoiding any decisions of a principled and binding nature, and passing legislation that provided a general framework, with details to be resolved on an ad-hoc basis.

From the time of its establishment, Mizrahi, which later became the National Religious Party (NRP), wielded power and influence in the religious councils and the Chief Rabbinical Council. In the period of the Mandate and during the first years following the establishment of the state, Mapai acquiesced to Mizrahi's exercise of influence. But when Mapai realized that the rabbis of the different immigrant communities exerted great social and political influence over their followers, they sought a decisive role in their selection and in the selection of members of religious councils. The change in Mapai's stance became evident in 1958 when the NRP resigned from the coalition on the first "Who is a Jew?" issue. Mapai took advantage of this opportunity to reduce the NRP's influence in the rabbinical and religious councils. The Ministry of Religious Affairs, which is the major governmental department with authority over the religious councils and which cooperates with the Chief Rabbinical Council, was transferred to the control of NRP opponents—an example of a change in the informal rather than the formal provisions of the status quo.

The struggle between the NRP and Mapai persisted even after 1959, when the NRP rejoined the coalition. The NRP resumed management of the Ministry of Religious Affairs only after elections to the Fifth Knesset in 1961, when its political influence rose. The two parties negotiated to determine how their influence over the Chief Rabbinical Council and the religious councils should be divided.

The issue of the rabbinical and religious councils illustrates how the absence of formal legislation permits a great deal of flexibility within the status quo agreement and how shifts in the balance of influence depend on shifts in the balance of power within the larger political arena.

The Religious Judicial System and Issues of Marriage and Divorce

At an early stage, the Knesset enacted laws that determined the authority and manner of elections of rabbinical court judges. The laws were based on the principles obtaining during the Mandate that provided rabbinical courts with exclusive authority over matters of marriage and divorce of Jews. Nevertheless, the new laws introduced a few changes. The most important one was the separation of the chief rabbis and local rabbinical officials from the rabbinical courts. The nonreligious parties demanded this separation, despite its deviation from the situation prevailing under the Mandate, in which the chief rabbis exercised authority over rabbinical courts. The religious parties felt compensated by the fact that Israeli law formally recognized that all matters of marriage and divorce of Jews were to be decided by religious law.

The principle of the status quo and the addition of the Knesset law means that religious control of marriage and divorce is fixed rather firmly. Nevertheless, there remains a great deal of controversy regarding the application of the law.[4] The Israeli Supreme Court exercises some technical authority over the rabbinical courts and hence can influence its decisions to some degree. In a few instances public pressure has led to more lenient decisions. But, for the most part, rabbinical courts have resisted outside pressures and the Supreme Court's capacity for intervention is severely limited by the law itself. Hence, any changes in the status quo arrangements affecting marriage and divorce would require new legislation. No serious effort in this direction has been undertaken.

Sabbath Observance

In 1948 the Knesset declared the Sabbath and Jewish holidays as legal days of rest in Israel, a declaration without operative authority. In 1951 the "Law of Working Hours and Rest" was passed. It obliged all Jewish employees to rest on the Sabbath and Jewish holidays but did not refer to the self-employed and members of worker cooperatives. The law also stated that work in factories or plants essential to the economy or to state security would be permitted on the Sabbath and holidays. A committee headed by the prime minister, minister of labor, and minister of religious affairs was formed to grant work permits.

The 1951 law was fairly limited in its effectiveness, but the religious parties were pacified by the commitment to maintain the status quo, that is, not to permit Sabbath work in those sectors of the economy which had not operated on the Sabbath and holidays during the Mandate period. For example, public transportation, except in Haifa, had not operated on the days of rest. Since the government itself supervised the cooperatives that operated the public transportation, no problem arose in this regard. Stores, businesses, places of entertainment, etc. were closed on the Sabbath in accordance with local ordinances, an authority also stemming from the Mandate period.

On this point as well, we see the tendency to refrain from legislating on sensitive matters of fundamental importance. Issues such as whether to operate cafés or places of entertainment on the Sabbath were transferred from the national to the local level. In this way a solution suitable to the balance of power in each locality could be reached. The problem was that Sabbath observance in a particular locality was dependent on the local coalition, which changed composition from time to time. The religious parties, therefore, demanded a national Sabbath law. Following the elections to the Third Knesset in 1955, Ben Gurion agreed that the government would present a Sabbath law to the Knesset. However, this law was never introduced because of differences of opinion as to what should be included in it. Mapai was willing to legislate the status quo, whereas the religious parties opposed any law that would sanction public transportation on the Sabbath and holidays in Haifa, one of Israel's three major cities. In addition, the NRP demanded that the minister of religious affairs be responsible for the execution of the law, while the labor parties insisted that the minister of labor be in charge. The controversy moved into high gear before the elections to the Sixth Knesset in 1965. Mapai entered the elections in an alignment with Aḥdut Ha'Avodah, a party to its left, which vigorously opposed any further concessions to the religious population. There was even opposition to legislation based on the status quo. The influential daily *Ha-Aretz* opposed the Sabbath law. Mapai now refused to agree to a Sabbath law, and instead submitted an amendment to the Law of Working Hours and Rest that obligated craftsmen and self-employed workers, stores, businesses, and places of entertainment to refrain from Sabbath and holiday work. The law, passed at the beginning of the Seventh Knesset, was basically consistent with the status quo.

Whereas in some areas the status quo is purely informal, many aspects of Sabbath observance are now protected by law. But overall, the public observance of the Sabbath in Israel has declined. The absence of a Sabbath law, economic pressures to operate on the Sabbath, and the authority of nonreligious ministers to grant work permits, have led to widespread

Sabbath violations. The nonreligious groups have been persistent in pressing demands for work permits, but they do not press their demands in ideological terms. For example, sharp controversy erupted in 1982 over the demands of religious parties, supported by Begin's government, that El-Al desist from operating on the Sabbath, a practice that had only begun in the late 1960s. Opponents of the change could have argued about the absurdity of a national carrier not operating seven days a week, about the inappropriateness of imposing laws of private religious observance on a nation-state, or about the fact that whereas Zionism had arisen as an effort to normalize Jewish existence, in this case Israel was emphasizing its peculiarity from the nations of the world. But, significantly, opponents based themselves on economic arguments about lost revenue to the state and to the El-Al employees accustomed to their overtime pay for Sabbath work.

In conclusion, the status quo agreement supplies a pragmatic resolution to religious-secular tensions and facilitates political partnership at the national level. The status quo is a dynamic solution: its provisions change delicately and subtly according to new balances of power and new circumstances. The principle, however, has remained constant since the establishment of the state.

— 4 —

The Dilemma of Reconciling Traditional Culture and Political Needs: Civil Religion in Israel

The agreement between the religious and secular camps, as the previous chapter indicated, has strong pragmatic overtones. It is based on the importance that both sides ascribe to maintaining national unity. It also reflects the political strength of the religious sector and their desirability as partners in a government coalition, although this second factor is of relatively slight importance.[1] But as suggested in chapters one and two, the agreement also emerges from the sense of the secular public that their loyalty to Israel is tied to their identification as Jews. To the extent that the secular public views the religious parties and rabbis as the caretakers, legitimate interpreters, or representatives of the Jewish tradition, they naturally seek to include them in all national forums. But we can, after all, conceive of a condition under which the secular public interprets Judaism in a manner quite distinct from the religious public. In fact, as we shall see in this chapter, such an interpretation existed in the past and is still held by a small minority today. This particular view has political as well as cultural consequences, stemming from the conceptions most Israelis share as to the purpose of the state.

There are two models or conceptions of the primary function of modern governments. We call one the service model. According to this model, the function of government is to provide services and to reconcile conflicting interests among different groups and individuals. David Apter uses the term "reconciliation system" to describe the "secular-libertarian" form of authority that generally characterizes such a state.[2] He contrasts it with what he calls a "mobilization system," characterized by a form of

---

This chapter is based on material from the authors' *Civil Religion in Israel: Traditional Religion and Political Culture in the Jewish State* (Berkeley: University of California Press, 1983). It appeared in slightly revised form in the October 1983 issue of *Comparative Politics* and in the 1983 *Yearbook of Political Anthropology*, ed. Myron Aronoff (New Brunswick, N.J.: Transaction Books).

authority based on a "sacred collectivity." This system fits, with some modification, what we call the visionary model. In this model, government has a predetermined vision or goal, and its primary function is to educate and mobilize the public on behalf of that goal. The term *vision* is appropriate since the goal transcends the immediate material needs of the nation's population, which is conceived of as a moral community.

Our models stand at two ends of a theoretical continuum and are useful in distinguishing between different governments that fall closer to one or the other end. Clearly the government of the Soviet Union or Nazi Germany or Cuba is closer to the visionary end of the continuum, and that of Sweden or England to the service end. But the service model is not necessarily more democratic, nor the visionary one more authoritarian. It depends to some extent on whom the government services and who generates and shares the vision (the elite or the entire population). There is a tendency for visionary governments to adopt authoritarian means, but this tendency may be restrained by other aspects of the political culture. Robert Bellah, for example, distinguishes a liberal-constitutional regime from a republic. Liberal constitutionalism (a service-type model) is built on the notion that "a good society can result from the actions of citizens motivated by self-interest alone when those actions are organized through proper mechanisms." The republic (a visionary-democratic–type model) "has an ethical, educational, even spiritual role. . . ."[3]

The foregoing suggests a four-celled matrix of modern nation-states (Table 1).

TABLE 1

Types of Modern States

	Democratic	*Authoritarian*
Service	A	B
Visionary	C	D

Type A, the service-democratic model, and Type D, the visionary-authoritarian model, are more common types of regimes but Type B, the service-authoritarian model (e.g., Jordan) and Type C, the visionary-democratic model (e.g., Israel) do exist in reality as well as in theory.

One would anticipate that any visionary government would develop a highly articulated system of symbols (rituals, myths, special terminology, shrines, heroic figures, etc.), which would define the boundaries and the meaning of the *moral* community, legitimate the vision, socialize the population to the values it embodies, and mobilize them to the efforts required for its realization. This system of symbols is what we mean by the term *civil religion.*

Civil religion, in turn, can be primarily political or social in its orientation.[4] Where the orientation is primarily political, the vision is generated and imposed by an elite, the symbols point to the centrality of the state, power and national unity are emphasized, and the structure of government tends to be authoritative, although as we shall see, even this orientation is compatible with a democratic regime.

Where the orientation is primarily social, the vision emerges as a collective conception and its parameters and meaning are defined by a variety of groups, each of which adds its own nuances. The symbols point to the society and its people rather than to the state, voluntarism and pluralism are valued more than power and unity, and the structure of government tends to be democratic rather than authoritarian.

Our concern is civil religion's approach to a problem endemic among all new nations: the relationship between the needs of the nation and the tradition(s) and culture(s) from which the new nation emerged. One can construct a civil religion out of new or syncretic symbols, denying any connection to a past tradition. There are problems with this option. Part of the population may be deeply committed to its own tradition and perceive it as bearing implications for the conduct of the nation. In addition the leaders of the new nation will want to exploit traditional symbols and values to strengthen national loyalties among this segment of the population. Furthermore, even among the more modern (secular) elements of the population, some primordial ties are likely to be retained, and the traditional culture offers the new nation a sense of continuity with the past. The tradition may serve to legitimate the people's rights to the land itself, to autonomy, and to an identity as a group distinct from others.

On the other hand, even if we assume only one tradition, some people may be ideologically as well as behaviorally nontraditional, if not antitraditional. Hence, traditional symbols may be divisive rather than integrative, delegitimating instead of legitimating. Second, values and behavior patterns anchored in traditional culture may hinder efforts to reorganize or make changes in the political, economic and social spheres.[5]

The problem is particularly acute in visionary-democratic states. Service states avoid the purposive shaping of their political culture. In the visionary-authoritarian state (all totalitarian states fall into this category), the political elite views the tradition, particularly when it is institutionalized in religion, as a competitor for loyalty and an obstacle to its effort to shape the society in accordance with its values. Hence, totalitarian regimes develop new symbols, which they hope will integrate and mobilize the population and legitimate their political vision. All the instruments of a modern state stand at their disposal in this effort. But under special conditions, in times of crises in particular, even totalitarian regimes may rely on traditional symbols. In that case they confront the dilemma of reconciling their political needs with the values inherent in traditional culture —a dilemma that visionary-democratic states confront most acutely since they lack the coercive instrumentalities of the authoritarian regime. The very condition of political freedom and the possibility of cultural pluralism make tradition an especially attractive source of symbols because of the deference in which it is held. This situation is particularly true where the majority of the population views itself as the heir of one tradition, and that tradition speaks in one way or another to matters of national concern. The dilemma arises, as we noted, when one or more dissenting minorities are present or when the traditional symbols and values are inappropriate to the political needs of a modern state. Hence we encounter the effort by democratic visionary states to transform and transvalue traditional symbols so that they become more compatible with the needs of dissenting minorities while fulfilling those of the state. Obviously, the problem can never be entirely resolved, since the more the symbols are transformed and transvalued to overcome one horn of the dilemma, the less "traditional" they become. Symbols are continually transformed and transvalued in traditional culture as well. The difference is in the degree and self-consciousness of the transformation and transvaluation. We distinguish three approaches or strategies of transformation and transvaluation in visionary-democratic regimes.

CONFRONTATION

In the first approach, the civil religion self-consciously confronts and to some degree rejects the tradition. But it forms its symbols out of this rejection. The link to the tradition is maintained by the very seriousness that is accorded to traditional symbols that have deliberately been changed in order to adapt them to new needs and values.

This approach is particularly suited to culturally sophisticated people among whom the tradition is too deeply embedded to be ignored but who have rejected many of its symbols and/or their referents.

It is not easy to sustain a confrontational approach in a pluralistic-democratic polity where a considerable part of the population is traditionalist. A civil religion that is based exclusively on such an approach is likely to be a divisive rather than an integrative force in society. Hence over the long run this approach can be maintained as one variant in a civil religion that makes room for other approaches or strategies as well.

SELECTIONISM

The second approach, which we call selectionism, maintains that the tradition is composed of a variety of strands reflecting different sets of symbols and values. Some of these are affirmed while others are simply ignored, rather than confronted and rejected. Selectivity, it is argued, is quite legitimate within the context of the tradition itself. In fact, some proponents of this approach claim that the part of the tradition that they affirm is really more legitimate, authentic, or essential than that which they reject.

This approach is associated with a system of beliefs and symbols that aspires to become the common civil religion of the whole polity. Such a civil religion tends to stress the importance of that which unites the nation, such as the state and its institutions. Hence, the selectionist approach is characteristic of a civil religion whose orientation is primarily political rather than social.

REINTERPRETATION

The third approach nominally affirms the entire tradition. The civil religion associated with this approach is characterized by the penetration of traditional symbols into all aspects of the culture and their reinterpretation so that new values may be imposed upon them. As we observed, all religious development is characterized by reinterpretation and the imposition of new values. The distinction is really the degree to which traditional symbols are reinterpreted to meet contemporary needs.

This approach is the least self-conscious of all and is closest, in structure as well as in content, to traditional religion. The attitude toward the tradition is very positive. Were the adherents of the reinterpretation approach to admit to their transvaluation of traditional symbols, they would transform them into arbitrary signs devoid of meaning and defeat the very purpose they seek to achieve: legitimating their values by linking them to the tradition. The reinterpretation approach is encouraged by a decline in the influence of modern-secular belief systems and in their capacity to legitimate societal institutions and values.

The Case of Israel

Israel is a visionary-democratic type society, and the nature of its vision makes the dilemma of reconciling traditional culture and contemporary political needs a two-dimensional one.

First, Zionism is the vision around which Jewish society in the land of Israel formed itself. According to this vision, Jews, through their own efforts, will construct a Jewish society in their own land, which will be the cultural and political center of all Jews. This is a basic component of Israeli civil religion in all its manifestations. In order to confirm the Jewish identity of the Israeli polity (and the polity of the *yishuv* before the establishment of the state), Zionist civil religion required symbols drawn from traditional Jewish culture that were capable of expressing and fostering the historic and contemporary links between Judaism, the Jewish people, and the Israeli polity.

As we have noted earlier, because of the central role of Jewish religion in the national history and culture of the Jewish people, there is hardly a single Jewish symbol that is not loaded with religious meaning. The problem with such symbols goes beyond the fact that broad circles in Israeli society are overtly secularist (these groups might simply accept the symbols as part of their historical heritage). The real problem lies in the references and meanings to which the symbols point. The Jewish religion is God-centered. It accords ultimate power and authority in human affairs, including those of a social and political nature, to God alone. God is the only true king of Israel, its sole protector and redeemer. It is not easy to reconcile this point of view with a conception of national self-redemption, which is a central component of modern Zionism.

This difficulty can be illustrated by reference to problems involved in the celebration of Jewish holidays. Passover and Hannukah (the Feast of Lights), two of the most widely celebrated Jewish holidays, have explicit national historical referents. Passover commemorates the Jewish exodus from Egypt; Hannukah, the Maccabean or Hasmonean revolt and the attainment of cultic freedom and a large measure of Jewish sovereignty in the Second Temple period.

Both these holidays, one might expect, would serve as important components of the Israeli civil religion, providing mythic-ritual symbols that would remind Israelis of their heroic past, their lengthy history, their ability in the past to overcome vicissitudes of fortune, etc. The problem is that the holidays have assumed a fairly specific meaning in the Jewish tradition, and subsymbols were developed or interpreted in accordance with this meaning. A central theme in the traditional meaning of both holidays is that success or victory was due entirely to God's miraculous intervention on behalf of the Jews and not to any action of the Jews themselves—not even of their leaders. As the traditional *haggadah* (pl.: *haggadot*), which Jews recite at the inception of Passover, states: "And the Lord brought us forth from Egypt, not by means of an angel, not by means of a seraph, not by means of a messenger: but the Most Holy, blessed be He, Himself, in His glory. . . ." Similarly, the meaning of Hannukah is conveyed in the prayer that Jews are instructed to repeat three times a day and following every meal during the holiday: "Then didst thou in thine abundant mercy rise up for them in the time of their trouble . . . thou delivered the strong into the hands of the weak, the many into the hands of the few . . . the arrogant into the hands of them that occupied themselves with thy Torah." What, according to the traditional liturgy, did the Jews themselves do? "After this, thy children came into the inner sanctuary of thy house, cleansed thy Temple . . . kindled lights . . . and appointed these eight days of Hannukah." The world view expressed in such a prayer is hardly reconcilable with a modern movement for national liberation.

The dilemma of reconciling Zionism and the tradition acquires a second dimension in the Jewish-Israeli culture. This is the problem of the relationship between those who settled in the land of Israel and the Jewish Diaspora, both past and present. Traditional Jewish culture, the Jewish religion, is primarily the product of two thousand years of Diaspora life. It bears the unmistakable imprint of a religious conception of reality and of a people that deemed itself powerless and homeless in material terms and compensated for this condition in symbolic terms. Zionism sought more than Jewish sovereignty in the land of Israel and the ingathering of the Diaspora; it called for the redemption of the Jewish people from their own tradition and culture, which Zionists perceived as a product of the unnatural condition under which the Jews had lived for so long. This perception involved a measure of hostility not only to the Jewish past but to the vast majority of Jewish people living outside the land who did not share the Zionist vision of immediate return to the land or self-sacrifice on behalf of the establishment of national independence. Exilic Jews were seen as passive, miserable, and oppressed, and the Diaspora a source of shame and humiliation.

On the other hand, since Zionism claimed to be acting on behalf of the Jewish people and as legitimate successor to the Jewish past, it could never dissociate itself from Diaspora Jewry and Diaspora culture. Israel, its existence as a state and its culture, is meaningful and significant to most Israelis precisely because they perceive it as the great achievement in the struggle of Jewish history, the culmination of longing embedded in Jewish culture, inseparably linked to the Jewish past and the Jewish people.

In the *yishuv* and the state of Israel, there were, and are, militant Jewish secularists who insist on total separation of Israeli society and culture from any link to traditional Judaism and to Jews outside Israel. At the opposite extreme are the ultrareligious, who deny the legitimacy of a so-called Jewish state that they perceive as the antithesis of authentic Judaism.

However, 94 percent of Israeli Jews affirm the attachment of Israel to Jewish peoplehood, culture, and history.[6] Among this vast majority of Israeli Jews, one can find proponents of each of the three approaches for reconciling traditional culture and contemporary political needs and values in Israel. One also finds among them a problematic group: the 12 percent who define themselves as religious and are committed to a Jewish state. Even the reinterpretation approach is not quite suitable to them. Their religious orthodoxy precludes their legitimating any transformation or transvaluation. Hence, they really stand outside Israeli civil religion. They evaluate each approach more or less sympathetically but never fully participate in any of them.

In the development of Israeli civil religion we can identify separate periods in which each approach was dominant, although one finds traces of all approaches in every period among different groups. We will associate each approach with the societal goals of the period in which it was dominant and illustrate how traditional symbols were transformed and transvalued in accordance with each approach.

Israeli civil religion has excluded the Arabs (15 percent of the total population). Their traditions (Christian-Arab, Muslim-Arab, Druze, or other) were never deemed relevant to the formulation of Israel's sacred symbols. Efforts to integrate Arabs into Israeli society have consisted of recognizing and legitimating their minority status with rights to partially autonomous cultures. The Jewish sector has sought to link them economically and politically, but not culturally or socially, to the larger society.[7]

Confrontation and Labor Zionism

As we noted, the confrontation approach is suitable to a culturally sophisticated group deeply rooted in the very tradition whose values it opposes and whose symbols may evoke a negative response. Confrontation was the characteristic approach of the Labor Zionist movement that led the *yishuv* in the two decades preceding the establishment of the state. While other strategies were present in that period, confrontation was the primary mode through which Labor Zionism related to the tradition and by which it developed a symbol system that both reflected and supported its particular values and perceptions of reality.

The Labor Zionist goal included the creation of a new type of Jew and a new society. Its very image of the desirable Jew and desirable society was the mirror image of the traditional Jew and traditional Jewish society. For example, Labor Zionism's attitude toward non-Jews and toward other nations was more universalist than that of the dominant civil religion of any other period. It deliberately rejected the particularism and ethnocentrism of the Jewish tradition.

We can see confrontationalism at work with regard to the old symbols, as traditional rituals and myths were deliberately inverted in order to accord with new needs and values. Whereas traditional Jews centered the celebration of the holiday of Hannukah on the cruse of oil that miraculously burned for eight days, a popular Hannukah song in the transformation period glorified the modern Zionist pioneers (really the *yishuv* itself): "we found no cruse of oil, no miracle was performed for us."[8]

The Passover celebration begins with a Seder or festive meal at which, as we noted, the *haggadah* is read. The kibbutzim formulated their own *haggadot*.[9] In general, God was excised, and nature, springtime, and nationalist elements were emphasized. Even revolutionary and class-struggle themes found expression in the *haggadot* of the more leftist kibbutzim. A most dramatic expression, however, of the confrontation approach is the statement by Ber Borochov (1881–1917), the foremost ideologue of the Labor Zionist movement. One of the most popular sections of the *haggadah* speaks of four sons: one wise, one wicked, one simple, and one childish. The second son is called wicked because he raises questions about the very basis of the Passover ceremonial and seems to exclude himself from the community of celebrants. Borochov, however, praised the wicked son, because that son wanted no part of the freedom given by God but insisted on attaining freedom by himself. The same "wicked ones," Borochov argued, are those who today insist on attaining freedom with their own hands and thereby create "the foundation for the construction of a new Jewish life."[10]

The strategy of confrontation is applicable to *new* myths and rituals as well. A striking example is the myth of Joseph Trumpeldor.[11] The story of Trumpeldor's death and the fall of Tel Ḥai in 1920 assumed mythic dimensions in the *yishuv* within a year of the event. From the very outset Trumpeldor was heralded as the archetype of the "new Jew." Even before his death Trumpeldor had achieved the status of a folk hero, noted for his courage. He was believed to be the first Jew appointed as an officer in the Czarist army. He was the antithesis of the "traditional Jew," who went to almost any lengths to avoid service in that army.

Comparisons between the defenders of Tel Ḥai and classical Jewish martyrs led Labor Zionist spokesmen to make invidious distinctions:

> The early martyrs all sought in return for their deeds . . . a place in the world-to-come—the personal pleasure which every religious Jew feels in giving his life. . . . This was not true of the martyrs of Tel Ḥai who did not sacrifice their lives for personal pleasure. . . . They were not concerned with whether or not they would earn pleasure in the next world. All that mattered to them was that the Jewish people should survive and the Land of Israel be rebuilt.[12]

According to another Labor Zionist spokesman, Trumpeldor, unlike Jewish heroes of the past, "is not merely a victim, a passive hero; he is an active hero." Finally, in what can only be seen as the adoption of antisemitic stereotypes, Trumpeldor was described as follows: "He had not a trace of sickliness, nervousness, impulsiveness, disquietude—qualities which characterize the Diaspora Jew." Ben Gurion declared that "for this generation"—those to whom he referred as "the comrades of Trumpeldor"—"this land is more holy than for the tens of generations of Jews who believed in its historical and religious sanctity; for it has been sanctified by our sweat, our work, and our blood."[13]

Although the civil religion of Labor Zionism was the most influential system of beliefs and symbols in the prestate period, it did not encompass the entire Jewish community. The religious sector opposed its overt secularism, and the Revisionists (ultranationalists) sharply criticized the socialist component of its belief system.

In a sense, there were several varieties of civil religion in the *yishuv* period, each with its own community of believers. The *yishuv* was in fact a federation of relatively voluntaristic and autonomous communities united by their common commitment to the Zionist ideal. Hence, the potential and even necessity for each to develop its own symbol system.

This situation changed after the establishment of the state. A politically oriented civil religion that strove to unite and integrate the entire Jewish population around the symbolism of the state now emerged. This symbol system, called *mamlakhtiut* (Statism), was associated with the selectionist approach, although it found its earliest development among the Revisionists in the prestate period.[14]

SELECTIONISM AND STATISM

Those traditional symbols which pointed to or could be interpreted as pointing to the centrality of the state were integrated into the civil religion; others were ignored. Ben Gurion and his followers defined and sought to impose their version of civil religion more explicitly than any other group of leaders in any other period. In the years from 1948 to the end of the 1950s Israeli civil religion assumed a political rather than a social orientation, almost meeting the criteria of political religion as Apter defines it.[15] Apter observes that political religion is particularly attentive to the young, in whom it places the hope for the creation of a new generation. It was to this group—a generation removed from firsthand encounter with the Jewish tradition and without the deep associations, memories, and nostalgia of their parents—that the statists projected their conception of the tradition.

Ben Gurion affirmed his unbounded admiration for some aspects of the tradition. On the other hand, he and other statists denied significance to that part of the traditional culture that originated in the period of Jewish exile. They posited the modern settlement of the land of Israel as the successor to the period of Jewish national independence, which ended in 70 C.E. The intervening two thousand years of exile were devoid of meaning.

The result of the exile, according to Ben Gurion, was to alienate the Jews from their greatest cultural achievement—the Bible. Postbiblical Judaism, he claimed, was apolitical, particularistic, and prone to exaggerated spiritualism. It neither understood nor properly appreciated the Bible and the biblical period, with its rich harmony of spiritual and material, moral and political, Jewish and universal values. Only those who had returned to their land and led an independent national life could truly appreciate the Bible. While Israel's first prime minister generally refrained from denigrating the rabbinic tradition, the product of the exilic period, his silence with respect to its literature, coupled with his reverence for the Bible and the biblical period, was enough. "We are consciously divorcing ourselves from the recent past," he wrote on one occasion.[16]

The Bible, in turn, was celebrated not only in the formation of adult study circles, or through the major emphasis given it in schools, or in the establishment of the international Bible quiz, which culminated on Israel Independence Day, but through fetishistic veneration, such as the creation of the Shrine of the Book, which houses the Dead Sea Scrolls.[17]

The most important new symbol reflecting the selectionist approach was Independence Day. We have defined selectionism as the affirmation of one strand in the tradition at the expense of others. How can such an approach incorporate new symbols? We argue that one can identify a strategy of selectionism when the new symbol is linked to a traditional one in such a way that one aspect of the tradition is emphasized at the deliberate expense of another.

In the early years of statehood an association was drawn between Independence Day and Passover, a link facilitated by the occurrence of the former thirteen days after the conclusion of the latter festival. There were many references in the first years of statehood to Independence Day, "the day of days," as a kind of culmination of the process that begins with the Passover celebration of the exodus from Egypt. Independence Day, therefore, replaced Shavuot, the holiday of the giving of the Torah, which was traditionally linked to Passover. The traditional paradigm was exodus (physical freedom) followed by the giving of the Torah (spiritual freedom). The new paradigm became exodus (freedom from foreign oppression by leaving Egypt) followed by Independence Day (achieving national autonomy by establishing the state). The paradigm was strengthened by comparisons between Ben Gurion and Joshua, who led the Jews into the Promised Land in the biblical period.

Reinterpretation and Israel's New Civil Religion

Neither Labor Zionism and its confrontational approach nor Statism and its selectionist approach maintained its dominant position in Israeli political culture. The massive influx of traditionally oriented immigrants following the establishment of Israel was one reason for the decline of the more secular civil religions. Indeed, the more secular the civil religion, the greater its difficulty in sanctifying institutions and patterns of behavior, because its symbols lack grounding in the collective consciousness and historical culture of the people. The more tenuously the civil religion is linked to the tradition, the more difficult it is to assert the sacred nature of its myths and rituals. David Apter found this to be true in authoritarian regimes.[18] It is certainly true in a democratic-visionary polity like Israel, where, as we have noted, the political elite cannot always draw upon the support of state-controlled instruments of socialization in order to maintain the total commitment of the population.

But the need remained for an ideational and symbolic system to legitimate the Jewish state, mobilize internal and external support for its survival and development, and provide its Jewish identity with content and meaning. The reasons behind the decline of Labor Zionist and Statist civil religions help account for the rise to dominance of the New Civil Religion, which utilizes the approach of reinterpretation and is more receptive to traditional culture and religion than the other two approaches.[19] The New Civil Religion reached a dominant position after 1967. Its influence peaked with the Likud victory in 1977 (the Likud is more closely identified with the New Civil Religion than any other party), though its roots are to be found in the mid-1950s, when the Jewish Consciousness Program was adopted for Israeli schools. Its goal was to unite and integrate the society around its conception of the Jewish tradition and the Jewish people; it no longer sought the creation of a new Jew and a new Jewish society (Labor-Zionism) or the unification and integration of the society around the symbols of statehood (Statism). However, the tradition and Jewish peoplehood, as we shall see, assumed a particular meaning in the New Civil Religion.

This is the most ethnocentric of all civil religions. It affirms all Jewish history and culture and gives special emphasis to the isolation of Jews and the hostility of Gentiles. The characteristic slogans of this period are the biblical phrase "a people that dwells alone" and the rabbinic metaphor "Esau hates Jacob." It is, needless to say, a civil religion especially well suited to masses who are familiar with and attached to traditional symbols but unsophisticated concerning their explicit meaning.

The tradition is reinterpreted—gently, subtly, and unselfconsciously. National motifs and a nationalist interpretation of religious symbols are omnipresent. A good example of this approach is found in the popular weekly army publication, *In the Camp,* which is intended for the average soldier and the general reader. It includes articles that relate specifically to the military but also devotes material to each holiday in the issue immediately preceding its onset. In a recent Passover issue, the cover reproduced a drawing from an 1849 *haggadah* showing Moses and the Egyptians at the Red Sea. Of the eight articles, three related to the holiday. One treated changes in the celebration of Passover in the kibbutz, stressing that the kibbutzim were now observing more and more of the traditional rituals. A second analyzed the character of Moses (lonely and isolated—note the parallel to Israel's contemporary self-image) and observed that "the most magnificent treatment of Moses, the most human and superhuman of all, and perhaps the most faithful to the truth, is that of the Torah." (The *haggadah,* it should be observed, never mentions

Moses, and the traditional reason offered is that there is only one hero in the exodus story, and that is God Himself). The third article recounted the 1920 Arab riots against Jews in Palestine, noting that they broke out on Passover.

THE HOLOCAUST IN ISRAELI CIVIL RELIGION

By definition one cannot create a new reinterpreted symbol, but the treatment of the Holocaust illustrates how the strategy of reinterpretation deals with a symbol of recent origin. Analysis of the Holocaust symbol also provides an instructive comparison of how each of the three approaches deals with the dilemma of relating the tradition (in this case the tradition of Jewish suffering and dispersion) to the needs of a modern state.

The very term Holocaust (capital H) is a symbol that points to the destruction of European Jewry. It has any number of other meanings and references according to how it is projected and interpreted. We cannot hope, in so brief an essay, to explore the problem of the development of the Holocaust symbol in Israeli society in any depth. Yet the different ways in which the symbol is projected and interpreted are so dramatic that they lend themselves to summary treatment.

As acute an observer of Israeli society as Amos Elon noted that Israelis "hardly give themselves the chance to forget the Holocaust. The traumatic memory is part of the rhythm and ritual of public life."[20] In the words of the army's *Informational Guidelines to the Commander,* the Holocaust to a great extent fashions "our national consciousness and the way in which we understand ourselves and the world in which we live."[21] In contrast to these observations it is significant to note that the mode of observance of Holocaust Day was only fixed in 1959, when the Knesset was called upon to act in the face of widespread public indifference to the day. Until then there were no visible signs of commemoration on the Israeli street. Places of entertainment operated as on any other day; there were no special radio programs. Hebrew writers simply ignored the Holocaust during the 1950s. Until the 1960s it found no expression in the school curriculum. It is true that in 1954 the government created Yad Vashem, a public memorial to honor the memory of the Holocaust victims. Today Yad Vashem is one of the country's two major shrines. But reading the Knesset debates surrounding its establishment, one senses how problematic the whole matter was to the leaders of Israel. The government only acted under pressure, not the least of which apparently was the fear that memorials would be established abroad, challenging Israel's status as the legitimate representative of the Jewish people, authorized to speak on behalf of all Jewry, including those who died in the Holocaust.

All this hesitation and reluctance reflected the selectionist approach, which chose to ignore traditional Gentile hostility. According to Ben Gurion: "German anti-Semitism, the Dreyfus trial . . . persecution of Jews in Rumania . . . they represent events from the past in foreign lands, sad memories of Jews in exile, but not emotional experiences and facts of life which educate and direct us."[22] In other words, this preoccupation was part of the tradition that the statists refused to incorporate in their symbol system. "The Jewish people erred when it blamed anti-Semitism for all the suffering and hardship it underwent in the Diaspora. . . . The cause of our troubles and the anti-Semitism of which we complain result from our peculiar status that does not accord with the established framework of the nations of the world. It is not the result of the wickedness or folly of the Gentiles which we call anti-Semitism."[23] According to Pinḥas Lavon, a member of Ben Gurion's cabinet and later minister of defense, the Holocaust is not without historical precedent. Jews, he said, were killed in the past. Furthermore, Nazi efforts at genocide had a precedent in the Turkish attempts to kill all the Armenians, "and the blood of the Armenian people is no less precious to them than ours is to us."[24]

The problem of the Holocaust symbol stemmed in part from the fact that the history of Diaspora Jewry and its condition as a persecuted minority was irrelevant to the statists. A second aspect of the problem was the Israeli perception of the victims' behavior as one of passivity and surrender—typical of exilic Jewry but one with which Israelis could not identify. Could one acknowledge this attitude without reopening wounds and destroying the unity of the Jews?

The confrontation approach, which we associated with Labor Zionism in the prestate period, faced this challenge squarely. The image of Holocaust victims who went "like sheep to the slaughter" was rife in the *yishuv*. According to one kibbutz *haggadah:* ". . . Hitler alone is not responsible for the death of six million—but all of us and above all the six million. If they knew that the Jew had power, they would not have all been butchered. . . ."[25]

But in the years following the end of the war, overwhelmed by the magnitude of Jewish persecution, by the presence of former concentration-camp inmates and European refugees in Israel, and perhaps by their own guilt in having judged the victims so harshly while doing so little to save them, the Israelis began a process of transvaluation, in which the Holocaust symbol now pointed to physical resistance and rebellion. In general it was the political left who remained faithful to Labor Zionist principles and a confrontation strategy, whereas the Labor Zionist right wing was attracted to Statism and selectionism. The former favored memorializing the Holocaust, and it was they who succeeded in imposing their symbolic model on the commemoration. What they did was to redefine the relevant behavior of the Holocaust victims to coincide with their own values, so that the victims became positive rather than negative role models. The day chosen by the Knesset to honor the victims was called "Memorial Day for the Holocaust and Ghetto Revolts" and was associated in particular with the Warsaw Ghetto uprising. Yad Vashem's subtitle was "Memorial Authority for the Holocaust and Bravery." Knesset members who favored its establishment (they included, we must add, Minister of Education Dinur, in other respects a leading advocate of Statism), connected the heroic acts of physical resistance against the Nazis with the heroism of Israeli fighters in the War of Independence.

But the Holocaust is commemorated today in the spirit of the reinterpretation approach. One finds references to bravery and resistance but this theme is not the major one. The Holocaust is primarily a paradigm for the condition of Israel and the hostility of its enemies. In the words of the present minister of education, ". . . the Holocaust is not a national insanity that happened once and passed, but an ideology that has not passed from the world, and even today the world may condone crimes against us." Contemporary values are, in retrospect, imposed on the past so that Israelis can derive the meaning they want from the past. The dead, for example, became victims who "sacrificed" their lives purposefully. According to the former president of Israel, "Our decision is firm that the people ingathered again in its ancient homeland will preciously guard these eternal values for which a third of our people sacrificed their life." Finally, the Holocaust symbol points to the debt that the world owes to Israel. According to a Knesset member speaking at the closing ceremony for Holocaust Memorial Day, ". . . even the best friends of the Jewish people refrained from offering significant saving help of any kind to European Jewry and turned their back on the chimneys of the death camps. . . . therefore all the free world, especially in these days, is required to show its repentance . . . by providing diplomatic defensive-economic aid to Israel."

– 5 –

Religious Orthodoxy's Attitudes toward Zionism

The first three chapters pointed to the interrelationship between religion and state built upon the need for national unity and the importance ascribed to Judaism as a component of national identity. Chapter four demonstrated, however, that Judaism can be interpreted as being at variance with the religious tradition. But today the religious tradition (albeit somewhat transformed and transvalued) is interpreted as entirely compatible with the society's needs. It constitutes the primary source of political symbols. But what about the other side of the coin? How do religious Jews interpret Zionism, the dominant ideology of Israel? How do religious Jews respond to the Zionist exploitation of the tradition? They respond in a number of different ways. We have seen what the Zionists have done to the older, more firmly embedded Jewish tradition, so it will not surprise us to find that at least one religious response was to transvalue Zionism itself. But to understand this and other contemporary responses we must look more closely at the historical background.

It is customary to distinguish two attitudes toward Zionism among Orthodox Jews: favorable and unfavorable. The favorable attitude is attributed to the National Religious Party (NRP), founded in 1956. (The NRP was created from the merger of Mizrahi, the international party of religious Zionism, founded in 1902, and Hapoel Hamizrahi, the religious labor Zionist party, an offshoot of Mizrahi.) The unfavorable attitude is attributed to Agudat Israel, which is part of the international organization of that same name, founded in 1912.[1] Sometimes a third attitude is distinguished, a more extreme, activist anti-Zionism, expressed by the

This chapter is based on an article by Eliezer Don-Yehiya that first appeared in Hebrew in *Hatziyonut* (1983).

Edah Ḥaredit and its most militant element, Neturei Karta, who refuse to participate in Israeli elections or recognize the legitimacy of the state.[2]

In fact, however, there has always been a range of attitudes toward Zionism among Orthodox Jews related to and depending in some measure on the definition of Zionism. Orthodoxy has perceived Zionism in three different though related ways, each of which evoked a distinctive set of attitudes: (1) Zionism as the practical effort to populate and settle the land of Israel, and the development of the economic and political infrastructure for this settlement; (2) Zionism as an organized movement encompassing religious and secular Jews in a cooperative effort to establish and assist a Jewish state (from the Orthodox point of view the problematic is the cooperation of nonreligious and religious Jews under the same organizational roof); and (3) Zionism as an ideology defining the meaning of Judaism, emphasizing the solidarity and mutual interdependence of the Jewish people by virtue of their national identity, common ethnic origins, language, culture, territory, and political allegiance.

ORTHODOX ATTITUDES IN THE PROTO-ZIONIST PERIOD

From the middle of the nineteenth century until about 1880[3] the controversy among Orthodox Jews was fairly low-key. The argument was primarily theological. It focused on the question of whether organized efforts to settle Jews in the land of Israel should be encouraged as signaling the *athalta d'geula* (the beginning of divine Redemption) and preparing the way for the coming of the Messiah, or discouraged because they constituted an effort to hasten the Redemption by human means, which, it was widely though not universally believed, were contrary to the religious tradition.

The controversy surrounded the publications and activity of Rabbis Zevi Hirsch Kalischer (1795–1874) and Judah Alkalai (1798–1878)[4] and their supporters. These men, known as the forerunners of Zionism, cited chapter and verse from rabbinical lore to prove that Redemption would come gradually and in its first stages would be effectuated by natural-human-rational means.

The Orthodox opponents of practical Zionism relied on the rabbinical tradition that prohibited any human-rational activity to hasten the Redemption. They labeled the organized effort to settle Jews in the land of Israel, to declare the Jews' rights to the land, and to establish any form of Jewish sovereignty over the land as *d'ḥikat haketz* (literally "pushing the end," i.e., bringing the end of days closer). According to a rabbinical tradition (whose legal authority some deny), God prescribed three oaths at the time the Jews were exiled from their homeland following the destruction of the Temple. One oath was that the Jews were not to "push the end," and another was that they were not to return to the land by force.[5]

Proponents and opponents of settlement relied upon other arguments as well, although these considerations were generally of secondary importance. Proponents spoke of settlement in the land of Israel as a means of improving the economic lot of impoverished Jews in the exile (Diaspora). They also emphasized the importance of fulfilling the religious commandment incumbent upon Jews to settle the land. Settlement, in turn, was a necessary condition to fulfilling other religious commandments connected with growing, harvesting and consuming agricultural products of Jews in the Holy Land. Opponents emphasized the economic and political difficulty of realizing any large-scale program of immigration and settlement.

Antisemitism played no role in the ideology of Zionism's forerunners. Zionist ideology after 1880, both secular and religious, reflects the conviction that the emancipation of the Jews had failed. In contrast, the proto-Zionists were responding to the promise and achievement of the political emancipation of Jews, in which they heartily believed. Their concerns were the problems of religious decline and assimilation that emancipation invoked.

The forerunners of Zionism, like the early religious reformers but unlike the bulk of traditional Jewish leaders, adopted a positive attitude toward emancipation. They sought to link it to the traditional vision of Redemption. The difference between reformers and proto-Zionists was that the former saw the emancipation as the realization of the messianic ideal. The value placed on integration into their surroundings became a substitute for the older vision of a return to Zion. Alkalai, Kalischer, and their followers saw the emancipation as a signal of the Redemption, which could only be fully realized by the return of Jews to Zion.[6]

The emancipation was associated with a rise in the economic status and political condition of the Jews. This improvement led some to believe that social equality and assimilation were now feasible options. It led the proto-Zionists, on the other hand, to seek national freedom, following the pattern of other nationalist movements in Europe. Finally, the secularizing and assimilationist consequences of the emancipation led the forerunners of Zionism to justify their program by arguing that Jews would reconstitute a traditional society in the land of Israel, insulated from the influences that were already undermining traditional religious belief and behavior in the Diaspora. This belief, in particular, was widely shared among religious circles (for example, among rabbinical leaders of Hungarian Jewry) whose members were not necessarily enthusiasts of the proto-Zionists' eschatological visions.

Orthodoxy and the Question of Cooperating with Secularists in the Hovevei Zion Period

The organization of Hovevei Zion (Lovers of Zion) in 1881, following pogroms in Russia, introduced a new element into the definition of Zionism.[7] Now there was a group engaged in settlement activity whose leaders and followers (the former in particular) included some who were not religiously observant. The controversy in religious circles became more widespread and heated than it had been heretofore, and it now centered on the propriety of cooperation with secularists. The theological controversy of the previous period was subordinated.

Among those who favored practical efforts toward immigration and settlement were some who opposed joint efforts with secularists. They pointed to the religious commandment prohibiting "cooperation with evil people." Other opponents stressed their fear of the influence of the secularists on religious members of Hovevei Zion. Finally, permitting nonobservant Jews to settle in the land was particularly wrong since the sanctity of the land of Israel rendered the violations of religious injunctions within its borders especially odious.

The Orthodox proponents of Hovevei Zion spoke of the positive value of cooperation among all Jews, particularly when the goal was settlement of the land of Israel. Second, they suggested the possibility that such cooperation would influence the nonreligious to repent. Finally, they relied on the practical argument that all resources had to be mobilized if efforts to build the country were to succeed.

The line dividing the sympathizers and opponents of Hovevei Zion was not sharply drawn. Even the preeminent religious leader within the organization, Rabbi Shmuel Mohliver (1824–98), expressed his dissatisfaction with the prominent role of nonreligious Jews among the leadership. Mohliver also waged a campaign against support for the Biluim, the only nonreligious but best known group of late nineteenth-century settlers in the land. Mohliver insisted that public support for settlements be conditional upon their members' observing a religious style of life.

Some Orthodox leaders supported Hovevei Zion at the outset but reversed themselves when stories filtered back that settlers whom the movement supported were violating religious laws. Other Orthodox leaders, torn between their support for settlement and Hovevei Zion's ambiguous attitude toward religion, refused to adopt any clear-cut position.

Those rabbis who continued to support Hovevei Zion were encouraged by the fact that the vast majority of its members were religious, as were most of the settlers in the land of Israel. In fact, the statutes of most of the early settlements required the members to behave in accordance with *halakha*. In addition, Hovevei Zion concentrated on support for practical activity in the land of Israel. There were those individuals and groups who espoused a secular Jewish nationalism, but the movement blurred the ideological aspects of Zionism and concentrated on practical efforts. This orientation facilitated cooperation between secularist and religious Jews in spite of the ideological antagonisms separating them.

The Rise of Ideological Factors in the Definition of Zionism

Zionist ideology began to assume an increasingly important role from the end of the nineteenth century. A nationalist-ethnic-cultural definition of Judaism increasingly challenged the traditional religious one. It was particularly insidious, many rabbis believed, because it borrowed so heavily from the religious tradition. There are a number of reasons for the growing importance of Zionist ideology and the elaboration of a new symbol system or the reinterpretation of older symbols in accordance with this ideology. The chief proponent of Jewish national culture was Ahad Ha'am (1856–1927), who was exceedingly influential among Zionist leaders.[8] Ahad Ha'am's publications and the organization of a select group of his followers (B'nei Moshe) drove a number of religious supporters of practical Zionist activity into the ranks of the Zionist opponents, thereby reducing their influence within Zionist circles and further strengthening the supporters of Ahad Ha'am. Second, the World Zionist Organization (WZO), established in 1897, which completely overshadowed Hovevei Zion, claimed to speak on behalf of the Jewish people. It necessarily expressed itself in modern nationalist terminology. Although it eschewed any cultural activity as long as Herzl led the movement and was sensitive to religious sensibilities, it imposed a nationalist definition on Judaism, if only by indirection. By virtue of Herzl's political activity to secure the assistance of the great powers in obtaining a charter for Jewish rights to a national homeland, the Jews were represented as a nation similar to other nations. Even before the WZO consciously undertook to do so, its actions encouraged the development of symbols that promoted a sense of Jewish national solidarity. Finally, the failure of Herzl's political efforts and the absence of any noticeable impact from practical attempts at settlement of the land encouraged many Zionists to turn their attention to cultural and educational efforts. They deliberately emphasized the ideological aspect of Zionism. From this point forward, the vast majority of Orthodox leaders perceived Zionism as an ideology foreign to and in conflict with traditional Judaism—the substitution of secular nationalism and concepts of territory, language, and political sovereignty for God, Torah, and the religious commandments.

According to the religious anti-Zionists, nothing good or useful can derive from heresy and secularism. Hence, even behavior that the tradition affirms loses its validity when it is uprooted from its religious source and associated with a secular world view. When based on feelings of nationalism rather than on religious belief, the identification with and concern for all Jews, or immigration into and settlement of the land, are unwelcome. Zionism was defined as *avodah zara* (worship of false gods), the most heinous of all crimes proscribed by the Torah. Rabbi Elḥanan Bunim Wasserman (1875–1941), one of the leaders of twentieth-century Orthodoxy, defined *avodah zara* as the belief that anything exists and can affect man independently of God's will.[9] Zionism, therefore, is a form of modern *avodah zara,* particularly dangerous because it was created by heretical Jews in rebellion against God.

Rabbi Moshe Blau (1885–1946), political leader of the non-Zionist Orthodox in the land of Israel, warned that the Zionists were more dangerous than the assimilationists, since the former are in revolt against the tradition whereas the latter are simply indifferent to it.

The Orthodox anti-Zionists extended their antagonism to religious Zionists as well. The latter were condemned not only for cooperating with secularists but for accepting the basic Zionist principle that attributes an ultimate and sacred value to nationalism. Religious Zionists were accused of adding this new value to the traditional values of faith in God and observance of Torah, that is, combining traditional Judaism and *avodah zara,* thereby transgressing the commandment "Thou shalt have no other Gods before me."

All the non-Zionist Orthodox circles shared a vigorous antagonism to Zionist ideology and to membership in the WZO. Most, but not all, supported Agudat Israel after its establishment in 1912. The non-Zionist

Orthodox, however, were divided in their attitude toward the practical efforts to settle the land and over cooperation with secularist Zionists on behalf of practical efforts outside the framework of the WZO.

The most vigorous opposition to Zionism, whether it is defined as practical effort, cooperation with secularists, or ideological commitment, comes, as we observed, from the Edah Haredit and Neturei Karta. They even condemn Agudat Israel for its passive rather than active opposition to the Zionist movement and their support for the state of Israel. Agudat Israel played an important role in the Likud government from the time of its accession to power in 1977, but particularly after its second victory in 1981. The most coherent reflection of the extremist ideology is found in essays by the late leader of the Satmar Hasidim, Rabbi Joel Teitelbaum (1888–1981).[10] The former Satmar leader and his disciples attribute demonic significance to Zionism in general and to the state of Israel in particular. In their view, the success and failure of Zionism and Israel are to be understood at a metaphysical level, and Jewish support for or opposition to Israel is of cosmological significance. As we shall see, the last two views have their analogues in the beliefs of the most vigorous proponents of religious Zionism, Rav Kook and his disciples. The intermediate positions, whether sympathetic or antagonistic to Zionism, tend to relate to it somewhat more pragmatically and in somewhat more muted theological terms.

Most of Zionism's opponents in the Orthodox community were antagonistic to its ideology and the fact that it was led by secularists but not to practical efforts toward settlement or, for that matter, to the establishment of a Jewish state. Some, in fact, were enthusiastic supporters of these efforts. When the WZO was founded, there were Orthodox Jews who joined despite their reservations about its secular cast. They hoped they could increase the role of religious Jews in the Zionist movement or at least prevent its adopting an ideology contrary to traditional Judaism. Some of them left the organization at an early stage. Orthodox leaders, mostly of the second rank, who didn't leave continued to struggle against the secularization of Zionist ideology. They organized the Mizrahi in 1902 as a faction within the WZO under the leadership of Rabbi Isaac Jacob Reines (1839–1915). Reines denied that Zionism was concerned with anything except the practical effort to improve the physical well-being of Jews.[11]

Unlike Reines, a number of Mizrahi leaders resigned from the WZO when it voted to engage in educational and cultural work in the land of Israel. Those who withdrew joined with other Orthodox Jews in forming

Agudat Israel in 1912. Hence, the ranks of Agudat Israel, from the outset, included some who were sympathetic to the practical efforts to settle and build the land of Israel.

An interesting and little-known effort by Orthodox opponents of the WZO to engage in practical Zionist work preceded the founding of Agudat Israel. In 1910, after a few faltering starts, a group of Orthodox rabbis led by Rabbi Mayer Lerner (1857–1930) of Altona, Germany, founded a society called Moriah, whose goal was the organization of observant Jews for efforts on behalf of settling the land of Israel.

Moriah's statement of purpose is of special interest because many of the most distinguished Orthodox rabbis of the period endorsed its goals. This declaration stresses the commandment of settling the land of Israel, a commandment that, readers are reminded, is equivalent to all other scriptural commandments and is directed to the Jewish public as well as to individual Jews. Jews are obliged, therefore, to undertake a collective effort to assist as many Jews as possible to immigrate to and settle in the land. The immigrants, in turn, will till its soil and make its wastelands flourish. Furthermore, settling Jews in the land of Israel represents a sanctification of God's name because it will result in Gentile recognition of the holiness of the land, of God's concern for it, and of the Jews' special attachment to it. The statement also notes that the revival of Jewish settlement in the land will resolve the material problems of many Jews who suffer in the Diaspora and ease the economic plight of the *yishuv hayashan* (the community of pious Jews, located primarily in Jerusalem, who constituted a majority of Jews in the land of Israel at that time and who opposed Zionist efforts toward settlement). According to Moriah, land would be purchased for these Jews, who would work it "by the sweat of their brow."

Membership in Moriah was only open to observant Jews. Its leader noted that the organization's importance stemmed from the joint efforts of "God-fearing Jews," under one organizational roof, to protect themselves from the influence of secularization and to strengthen the role of religion in private and public life.

The declaration refuted the argument that mass immigration violated the religious prohibition of taking the land by force. Even if it is believed that this prohibition is a matter of *halakha* rather than homiletical, it declared, there is no objection to massive settlement since only the taking of the land by force of arms is prohibited.

Moriah's leaders obviously intended to create an organization of religious Jews to rival the WZO. Mizraḥi's attitude, as might be expected, was ambivalent. A number of Moriah branches were established in Eastern Europe. However, the establishment of Agudat Israel as the organized voice of the non-Zionist Orthodox world, with the support of the leading rabbinical figures of the period, inhibited the growth of Moriah. In 1930 Agudat Israel absorbed it.

AGUDAT ISRAEL AND ZIONISM

Agudat Israel opposed ideological Zionism and the WZO but not practical Zionism. Over the course of its history, it adopted a variety of resolutions calling for practical and political efforts on behalf of settling the land and establishing a dominant Jewish presence there. Agudat Israel's support for such efforts (which until the pre–World War II period was hardly more than paper support) was justified in terms of easing the economic plight of Diaspora Jews. But Agudat Israel also recognized the importance of the religious commandment to settle the land. However, a small minority conceived of building the country as a project of national-religious and even messianic significance, a dimension absent in the thinking of the majority of Agudat Israel's leaders.

The leading proponent of this position was Isaac Breuer (1883–1946), one of the founders of the organization.[12] Breuer, "the Zionist who fought Zionism," inveighed against ideological Zionism, which he perceived as a revolt against the sovereignty of God. He bitterly opposed participation of religious Jews in any Jewish organizational framework that didn't accept the authority of Torah. On the other hand, Breuer saw in the Balfour Declaration (1917) and the renewal of Jewish settlement in the land evidence of the beginning of Redemption, and he demanded that Orthodox Jewry center its efforts on establishing the land of Israel as a national home for Jews who are faithful to Torah.

Breuer contrasted Zionism, which affirms the sovereignty of the nation as its central tenet, with "Torah nationalism," whose central tenet is the sovereignty of God and Torah. The "nation of Torah," he believed, will establish the "state of Torah," not the national state that the Zionists envisioned. Breuer's position found few supporters within Agudat Israel. His conceptions of the redemptive messianic role of the return to the land together with his bitter opposition to those who were, in fact, engaged in that enterprise were difficult to accept.

In the 1930s, Agudat Israel moderated its opposition to the WZO and cooperated with its leadership on a limited basis. Agudat Israel's leaders were impressed by the practical successes that the Zionists had registered.

Breuer's vision to the contrary notwithstanding, Agudat Israel found it could not accomplish very much in the land of Israel without the cooperation of the secularists. These developments took place in the context of rising antisemitism and economic dislocation among Eastern European Jews (in Poland in particular), where the core of Agudat Israel's supporters lived. The organization had little to offer their supporters in material terms, and the Zionist solution was increasingly attractive to the masses of religious Jews. Finally, the Holocaust, the destruction of the centers of Jewish population and culture in Eastern Europe, the transfer of many of the survivors to the land of Israel, and the establishment of the state of Israel itself, strengthened that wing within the organization which sought active participation in the building of the Jewish state.

Agudat Israel never joined the WZO and continued to reject Zionist ideology. But its attitude toward the state of Israel was much more positive. Israel imposes the authority of its law but not a particular political ideology. Hence, Agudat Israel found itself able to support Israel's existence and participate in its institutions without presumably compromising its commitment to Torah, a position that its more religiously extreme opponents in the Edah Haredit vigorously reject.

From all we have said, it appears that the common denominator of non-Zionist Orthodoxy is the opposition to Zionist ideology and, as a consequence, refusal to participate in the WZO. The common denominator among religious Zionists is the affirmation of practical Zionist activity and, as a consequence, a willingness to cooperate with secularists and participate in the WZO. Religious Zionists were anxious to stamp the mark of traditional religion on the institutions of Zionism but, unlike the non-Zionists, they did not condition their cooperation with the secularists on that basis.

Religious Zionism at the Crossroads

Some religious Zionists, the more serious thinkers in particular, felt obliged to confront the problem of Zionism's secular basis. Secular Jewish nationalism assumed increased importance in the Zionist movement, as we have already noted. Within the *yishuv*, in particular, the settlers sought to infuse meaning and significance into their enterprise. They were not satisfied with defining their activity in terms of the satisfaction of their material needs, and it was quite natural that Zionism developed into a quasi-religious system within the *yishuv*.[13] This, in turn, presented religious Zionists with a serious problem. Zionist ideology was inconsistent with the religious tradition as it was understood. This left religious Zionists with four options. The first, represented by Rabbi Reines, was to deny any ideological content to Zionism. The second, represented by Rav Amiel, was to acknowledge the ideological antagonism and encourage joint efforts in practical Zionist activity despite this antagonism. The third, represented by Rav Kook, was the reinterpretation of Zionist ideology in the spirit of the religious tradition. In fact, this approach also involved reinterpreting the religious tradition by expanding its scope to areas heretofore considered as secular. The fourth option, represented by *Torah v'avoda*, was a reinterpretation of the religious tradition in order to adapt it to Zionist ideology. The first two options meant that cooperation between religious and nonreligious Zionists would be based on purely pragmatic grounds. The last two options involved far deeper levels of cooperation and were associated with messianic interpretations of Zionism.

ZIONISM AS A NONIDEOLOGICAL MOVEMENT

Rabbi Reines objected to any legitimation of secular Judaism based on language or culture. He certainly objected to substituting the vision of national independence for the religious vision of messianic Redemption, although he saw the nationalist awakening among nonreligious Jews as evidence of their return to the tradition. His desire to cooperate with the secularists within the WZO was based primarily on the utilitarian calculation of the best means to realize the Zionist goal of resolving material problems of Jewish life. Zionism's answer, according to Reines, was to create a "secure haven" for Jews by obtaining international recognition for their right to settle in the land of Israel and to establish an autonomous government there. Therefore, argued Reines, nothing in Zionism constituted a substitute for traditional Judaism, nor did Zionism threaten traditional Judaism. When in 1911 the Tenth Zionist Congress adopted a program of cultural activity, he insisted that this resolution was a distortion of Zionism. He realized that some Zionists conceived of the movement in broad ideological terms, but he sought to minimize their importance and influence.

Reines's conception of Zionism contrasted with the messianic-redemptive element central to Kalischer and Alkalai's vision. They represented the Zionist awakening as evidence of the beginning of Redemption. But a few decades later, in Reines's time, such a conception would have meant defending the notion that Israel's redemption would proceed from the activity of those who desecrated basic religious commandments. Rav Kook, as we shall see, was prepared to offer just such a defense. But it was certainly more practical and sensible for less imaginative minds to defend Zionism in Reines's terms.

Reines and his followers were particularly enthusiastic supporters of Herzl. Herzl backed their early organizational efforts, and most of them sided with him in support of his Uganda proposal, a proposal not inconsistent with Reines's desire to obtain a "secure haven" in an enterprise bereft of higher religious meaning or significance. (Herzl's recommendation was that the WZO consider Great Britain's offer to explore the possibility of Jewish settlement and a measure of autonomy in a portion of eastern Africa mistakenly called "Uganda." The proposal won a small majority at the WZO Congress of 1903, but opponents were so bitter that it became clear to Herzl and most of his supporters than an honorable way to bury the proposal would have to be found.)

The problem with Reines's position was that by the second decade of the century it was clear that, regardless of how he defined Zionism, the majority of the movement saw it in different terms. Furthermore, Reines's definition was unsatisfactory to religious Zionists themselves, who preferred to believe that the enormous effort involved in settling and building the land of Israel was of religious significance. In fact, most of them, particularly those in the labor wing of Mizraḥi, were religious rebels of a sort and associated their immigration to the land of Israel with their own opposition to the religious establishment of Eastern Europe. They believed that as Orthodox Judaism developed in the land of Israel it would take on new dimensions. On the other hand, if Zionism was of religious significance, how could religious Zionists continue to cooperate with secularists within the framework of the WZO, when it was increasingly apparent that the latter's ideology, symbol system, and cultural activity served as functional substitutes for traditional Judaism?

Lest we be misunderstood, it should be stated that many and perhaps most religious Zionists may have never thought about or been troubled by these questions. But two leading figures did direct their intellectual efforts to their resolution. One of them, Rav Amiel, had little influence over religious Zionism, no doubt because the consequences of his position were too radical at the time he proposed it. The second, Rav Kook, a far more religiously radical thinker than Amiel, exercised enormous influence, in part, at least, because the practical consequences of his position led religious Zionists to do what suited them for purely pragmatic reasons. Paradoxically, as we shall see, Rav Kook's thought as further developed by his son, Rav Zvi Yehuda Kook (and by his contemporary disciples in

Gush Emunim) led to the most radical consequences of all for religious Zionism.

Religious Zionism as the Antagonist of Secular Zionism

Rabbi Moshe Avidgor Amiel (1882–1946), chief rabbi of Tel-Aviv from 1936, was aware of the contradiction between the nationalist conceptions of secular Zionism and those of religious Judaism. Rav Amiel cautioned against statements of Mizraḥi spokesmen from which listeners might infer that the only difference between religious and nonreligious Zionists was that the former were both religious and Zionists. The central question, according to Amiel, was not the addition of religion to Zionism but the basic meaning of Zionism, its essence and its goals. Religious and nonreligious Zionists, he argued, shared nothing in common ideologically. The desecration of religion by the settlers in the land of Israel stemmed, he maintained, from the core definition of Zionism.

Judaism commands the settlement of the land as a religious obligation. Zionism, in contrast to authentic Judaism, is a form of secular nationalism without a theological or, for that matter, a universalistic base. Judaism always retains a universalistic element, since the God of Israel is God of all the world. The Zionists undermine this universalism by focusing exclusively on the land of Israel and the Hebrew language. Furthermore, secular nationalism is immoral, since it projects the importance of power rather than righteousness.

Rav Amiel denied the idea that because Zionism identified itself with selected values and symbols of the tradition this signaled the secularists' return to religion. The identification, he felt, was not a retreat from secularism, but an effort to legitimate Zionism by clothing it in the mantle of tradition. Secular nationalism is worse than secularism without a nationalist component.

Amiel's opposition to Zionist ideology sounds very much like that of Agudat Israel. But Amiel believed that it was legitimate to cooperate with the nonreligious Zionists on behalf of the practical effort to build the country, though not in any cultural or educational effort. Indeed, he favored a reevaluation of Mizraḥi's membership in the WZO and increased cooperation with Agudat Israel to unite all religious Jewry to build the land of Israel in the spirit of Torah.

Rav Amiel's criticism of Zionism was published in 1934, when relations between the WZO executive (under control of Mapai since 1933) and religious Zionists were at their nadir. This factor helps explain the popularity of his recommendations. But in 1935 Mizraḥi reached an agreement with Mapai, which lasted until Mapai's successor, the Labor party, lost its dominance in the WZO and in the state of Israel to the Likud in 1977. Mizraḥi's representatives joined the Zionist executive, and a number of controversial issues surrounding the public observance of religion in the *yishuv* were resolved. One result was weakened support for Rav Amiel's position. People turned instead to the search for an ideology that legitimated full cooperation between religious and nonreligious Jews on an ideological as well as a pragmatic basis. Amiel's position meant the isolation of religious Zionism. The alternative was a reinterpretation of either Zionist ideology, the religious tradition, or both in order to demonstrate that they were not contradictory. We will devote our attention to the most intellectually important effort in this regard, that of Rav Kook and his followers. Rav Kook reinterpreted both Zionist ideology and the religious tradition, but he was more radical in his reinterpretation of the former.

ZIONISM AS A RELIGIOUS MESSIANIC PHENOMENON: THE PHILOSOPHY OF "EXPANSIONISM"

Rabbi Abraham Isaac Kook (1865–1935) was the first chief rabbi in the land of Israel elected under procedures approved by the British mandatory power.[14] Rav Kook confronted the problem of a Zionist movement led by secularists committed to an ideology in apparent contrast to a religious world view. Yet, he believed, Zionism was a movement intimately associated with messianic Redemption. Rav Kook's answer to the question of how "Redemption could be wrought by evil people" was part of his effort to explain the growth of secularism and heresy among Jews and in the world precisely in the period when signs of Redemption had appeared.

Rav Kook borrowed heavily from concepts of the Jewish mystical and homiletical literature. But he added his own interpretation of these concepts. A term he frequently relied upon was *ikvita d'meshiḥa* (footsteps of the messiah). This phrase refers to the period immediately preceding the Redemption, which is generally described as a time of material and moral decline. In representing the contemporary period as one of *ikvita d'meshiḥa,* Rav Kook relied on traditional Jewish sources to prove that secularism and heresy, which his generation witnessed, point to the coming of the messiah.

Nevertheless, how was one to justify cooperating with secularists? The interesting point here is that the late leader of Satmar Hasidim and Rabbi

Elkhanan Wasserman also felt that their period was one of *ikvita d'meshiḥa*. But this conviction only proved to them that the Zionist organization was not a movement of Redemption but an expression of arch evil. As far as they were concerned, Redemption would arrive as the antithesis of secularism. Redemption signals the victory of absolute good; *ikvita d'meshiḥa* is the rule of evil that seeks to hinder the coming of Redemption.

In contrast, Rav Kook finds continuity between the periods of *ikvita d'meshiḥa* and Redemption, despite their obvious differences. This conclusion is consistent with his dialectical scheme, in which Redemption occurs not as the reversal of all that preceded it but as the zenith in the evolution of mankind toward its ultimate, preordained goal.

How is this evolution to be squared with the evidence of moral and spiritual decline among Jews as well as the nations of the world? Rav Kook's answer lies in his distinction between internal and external manifestations. Redemption, following the Jewish mystical tradition, is really the reuniting of the cosmos with its divine source, from which it was alienated at the time of creation. This "cosmic alienation" is not total. Indeed, no aspect of reality is entirely separated from its divine origin, whose stamp is found everywhere and which is the source of all that is good. However bad or evil a phenomenon may appear, there is some good inside it stemming from its orientation to the divine.

The evidence of heresy among Jews and non-Jews is an outward, superficial manifestation, which is unable to impede the progress toward Redemption. This progress is expressed in the awakening of the inner sense of association with the divine and the urge to do that which is just and right. The awakening can be quite unselfconscious, and those who participate in it may be unaware of its true source. It can be misinterpreted as the awakening of natural or moral emotions unconnected to religious consciousness. Hence, it comes as no surprise that we find individuals and groups infused with a national and moral spirit, working on behalf of their people or all humanity, yet declaring war on God and His word. In fact, their acts stem from the emergence of the "divine spark" in their souls. But they do not realize this because the spark is buried so deeply in the inner recesses of the soul.

The contrast between inner and outer manifestations is particularly sharp at the threshold of Redemption. Rav Kook cites proof texts from rabbinical lore to buttress this assertion, but he also relies on less metaphysical arguments. The development of Judaism and all mankind, he argues, is associated with the broadening of knowledge, understanding, and consciousness and is therefore connected to sharpened critical insights and a revolt against custom and convention. In the early stages of human development, simple unquestioned, unexamined faith was rife. The development of human intelligence undermined this simple faith. But this early stage of religion, which is now undermined, is itself a sign of undeveloped religious consciousness. As the intellectual and moral capacities of mankind develop, new heights of faith and service to God will be reached. As the time of Redemption approaches, the contrast between inner and outer manifestations recedes, the inner absorbs the outer, and the orientation of all creation to its creator becomes evident.

According to Rav Kook, the Redemption of all mankind is directly related to the Redemption of the Jewish people, and all that Rav Kook says of Redemption in general applies to the Jews. All people are partners in the task of exposing the sparks of holy light hidden behind the outward façade of secularism. All must engage in extending the influence of the holy to all areas of private and public life. But Jews have a greater responsibility, since all that is good and holy stems from and is influenced by the special qualities that constitute the spiritual essence of Judaism, which has a special affinity and orientation to its divine origin.

Rav Kook perceives Jewish national identification, the willingness of the Zionist settlers to sacrifice themselves for the Jewish people and for the land, as a phenomenon of major religious significance. Although the settlers deny that they are religiously motivated and often violate religious commandments, they are nonetheless protagonists in this important religious event. "The nation of Torah" (a phrase borrowed perhaps from Breuer) is not limited, according to Rav Kook, to those who consciously observe the Torah. Anyone born Jewish is identified with Torah and its divine origin, even if he does not yet recognize this fact. National awakening, Rav Kook claimed, stems from a holy source and points to the coming repentance of nonobservant Jews.

Jewish national revival is not limited to the return to the land of Israel and the reestablishment of Jewish sovereignty. The essence of the national revival is to break out of the confines and self-imposed isolation that characterized Jewish life in the Diaspora, to encompass broad areas of life that were heretofore ignored.

On this point, Rav Kook's conceptions resembled those of secular Zionists, settlers in the land of Israel in particular. The Diaspora, or "exile" as it was more frequently called, was conceived of not only as a condition of oppression but as a cultural-spiritual experience characterized by detachment, isolation, contraction, divisiveness, distorted spirituality, and alienation from nature and creativity. The "national revival" represented a return to nature and creativity, the cultivation of aestheticism, heroism, and the renewal of the forces of life among individual Jews and the Jewish collectivity.

However, unlike the secular Zionists, Rav Kook did not attribute the negative aspects of Diaspora life to the religious tradition. Judaism, he argued, is characterized by the desire to encompass all of life and to imprint the stamp of holiness and divinity on all objects and experiences. Thus, the Zionist enterprise is a true expression of the essence of Judaism, even if the Zionists themselves fail to recognize it. The attributes of nationality that are so dear to the Zionists—language, land, history, custom —are all infused with the divine spirit. The exile, which detached the Jews from their land also resulted in the detachment of the holy from the day-to-day material aspects of life. True, this condition also characterizes other nations and is reflected in all human experience. The difference is that whereas other nations live in their own land, conduct their own affairs, develop their own economies, but lack a spiritual dimension to their lives, the Jews lack a material dimension. As a result, the spirituality and sanctity that they possess in abundance is one-sided and detached. Diaspora life is characterized by the contraction of Jewish national existence to matters of religion and spirit, and alienation from other facets of existence.

This detachment is unnatural, though it stems from conditions necessary for Jewish survival in the Diaspora. The absence of territory required Jews to formulate their national life with exclusive regard to the spiritual. In addition, this orientation was their only defense against threats to the Jewish spirit stemming from living in countries where materialism was rampant. The excessive spirituality of Diaspora life was also attributable to the fact that the exile originally came as punishment for the sin of excessive materialism. Hence, the Jews had to overcompensate.

The national revival includes a revolt against the exile. It is to be welcomed, even when accompanied by an unfortunate corollary. The reaction to the excessive spirituality of the immediate past has evoked the tendency among Zionists toward an exclusive concern with material matters, and the apparent weakening of the element of holiness. In addition, any revolt or radical change, even when directed against negative manifestations, is associated with the destruction of existing frameworks and structures.

Although one can explain the manifestations of heresy and secularism in Zionism, it does not mean that religious Jews ought to resign themselves to it, according to Rav Kook. Religious Zionists are obliged to do everything possible to bring those engaged in the Zionist enterprise to a recognition that the value of their work is in its dependence on the eternal tie between the Jewish nation and the land of Israel on the one hand, and the God of Israel and His Torah on the other. Cooperation with secularists in the work for national redemption is therefore of positive value. It will hasten their recognition of the true nature of their motivation and goals and will encourage them to return to God and Torah.

The renewal of independent national life, in turn, will permit the fullest expression of the national spirit and the sanctification of all areas of life, since the national spirit will be guided by the Torah. According to Rav Kook: "In general the state is like a society for mutual responsibility. It is certainly not the greatest happiness of man. . . . But this is not true of a state whose existence inscribes the noblest ideals of man. . . . Such a state is truly the greatest happiness and such a state is our state of Israel . . . whose only wish is that God shall be one and His name one, which is truly the greatest happiness."[15]

Most of Rav Kook's work was published posthumously, after undergoing editing and, some believe, censorship by his son and his disciples. But most of the material was written in the earlier stages of his career, forty to fifty years before the establishment of the state of Israel. After 1948 many of Rav Kook's followers applied his philosophy of expansionism to the state itself and its institutions. The state became the concrete expression of Redemption.

The most influential group of Rav Kook's followers gathered around the Yeshiva Merkaz Harav, which he had established. His son, Rav Zvi Yehuda (1891–1982), whose intellectual capacity was hardly the equal of his father's, emerged as the leader of this group. His influence over his followers was to exceed the influence his father exercised, perhaps because Rav Zvi Yehuda was far more specific about the political and behavioral implications of his doctrine. Unlike his father, Rav Zvi Yehuda wrote very little. His ideas were expressed in lectures and discussions, the most important of which were published by his disciples in two volumes in 1969.[16]

In a speech delivered two months before the Six-Day War, Rav Zvi Yehuda called the establishment and existence of Israel an expression of Redemption and the fulfillment of a religious commandment of the highest order. But how can the state and its institutions express divine Redemption when they are of a secular character? The answer is that sanctity is unconditionally granted to Jews and their land; according to Rav Zvi Yehuda, that is the nature of a holy object: it can never be desacralized. God ordained the Jews and the land of Israel as holy. The difference between Rav Kook and his son, in this regard, is a subtle one but has enormous practical consequences. The father spoke of the task of actualizing the holiness embedded within the Jewish nation by directing its actions in accordance with the Torah. He emphasized that as the process of Redemption unfolded, the movement for the repentance of Jews, their return to the faith of their fathers, would become evident, and everyone would witness the light of divine holiness in the Jewish people. In the son's conception, the emphasis is on the existence of the Jewish state and its achievements in the political and economic realms. Whereas Rav Kook, as we already observed, spoke of the state as the "supreme happiness of man," his reference was to an idealized state of Israel. His son stressed the sanctity of Israel as a real state. Indeed, Israel plays so central and sanctified a role in his conception that he speaks of the "real Israel" as opposed to Diaspora Jewry. "The real Israel is the Israel which is redeemed: the kingdom of Israel and the army of Israel, a whole nation and not an exilic Diaspora."[17]

Zvi Yehuda accords a major role to the "commandment of conquest" that obliges the use of armed force for its fulfillment. Its purpose is to protect Jewish sovereignty over the land of Israel. This is why he attributes sanctity to Independence Day parades, in which the army demonstrates its armed power. "With this power we must fulfill the commandment incumbent upon us—conquest of the land. . . . Therefore, everything connected to it, all forms of weapons, whether produced by us or by the Gentiles, everything associated with this day of the establishment of the kingdom of Israel—all is holy."[18]

The "commandment of conquest" extends to the entire territory promised by God in the Torah. Hence, the vigorous opposition to any territorial compromise, a position enunciated even before the creation of the state and with increased vehemence and greater political resonance after 1967. Since Jewish sovereignty over all the territory of the land of Israel is an explicit sign of the Redemption, any compromise or retreat represents an interruption and delay in the process of Redemption.

A readiness to compromise and cooperate with other nations is also seen as a serious assault on Jewish national pride. This attitude is part of Rav Zvi Yehuda's general position, which emphasizes the distinctive nature of the Jews and the absence of any connection between Jews and other nations. To secular Zionists, particularly in the prestate period and the first few years of statehood, Jewish national redemption meant emergence from the isolation in which Jews had lived and participation as equal members of the community of nations. In opposition to this vision, messianic religious Zionism of Rav Kook's variety stresses the unique status of the Jewish people. The very creation of Israel, which Zionism saw as the normalization of Jewish existence, is viewed by messianic religious Zionism as the insulation of the Jewish people, accomplished by transferring them to their own isolated cultural and political structures. Whereas the exile is characterized by mixing of Jews and Gentiles, the Redemption is signaled by their separation from Gentiles, the reuniting of Jews in their own land. Rav Kook emphasized the sanctity of the Jewish nation and the divine attributes imprinted on it, but he also gave expression to a form of universalism reflected in the idea of Jewish obligations to the rest of the world or the fact that the national redemption of the Jews was a condition and first stage in the Redemption of all humanity. Rav Zvi Yehuda, on the other hand, stresses the contrast between Jews and all other nations. His point of view reflects the experience of the Holocaust, which he sees as evidence of the evil of the Gentiles and the deep chasm and abiding hatred separating them from the Jews. His conclusion is that Jews must not put any trust in Gentiles or consider their opinions. The Jews must act on their own, considering only their own interest, placing their faith only in God.

The political implication of Rav Zvi Yehuda's thought helps explain his particular relevance to and influence upon broad sectors of the religious Zionist public after 1967 and especially after the 1973 Yom Kippur War. His influence was particularly notable within Gush Emunim, (to be discussed in chapter seven), founded in 1974. Some of its leaders were students in Merkaz Harav. But Zvi Yehuda was adulated as a spiritual leader by many in Gush Emunim outside of Merkaz Harav circles, including many who were nonreligious. In all likelihood they never read his articles or heard his speeches, or understood them if they did. His language and delivery were most difficult to comprehend, especially to those unfamiliar with the particular rabbinic style in which Zvi Yehuda expressed himself. But the outlines of his thought and its political implications were popularized by some of his closest students and aroused positive echoes among militant Jewish nationalists of all types.

RELIGIOUS ACCOMMODATION TO ZIONIST IDEOLOGY

The final effort to synthesize Zionism and Judaism that invites attention, less because of its intellectual distinction than because it represented the position of most religious Zionists until the 1960s and 1970s,[19] is the adaptationist position. Its dominant expression is found in the ideology of *Torah v'avoda* (Torah and labor), adopted by Hapoel Hamizrahi, the religious Zionist labor party, which is also sometimes referred to as *Torah v'avoda*. The most forceful exponents of the ideology were to be found in the religious kibbutz movement.[20] *Torah v'avoda*, in contrast to Rav Kook, places the weight of its synthesis on reinterpreting the religious tradition. The typical *Torah v'avoda* position is expressed, for example, in the statement that "religious Zionism always believed that it is possible to maintain a modern developed state in accordance with the *halakha* . . . but we also knew that this implies the confrontation of the *halakha* with a changing reality and hence with the renewal of the *halakha* in all areas of life, especially in the public-governmental realm."[21] This type of statement reflects the willingness of *Torah v'avoda* to adapt or reinterpret the religious tradition to contemporary needs, although, in practice, virtually no halakhic changes were introduced because no rabbinical authority ever sanctioned them.

Torah v'avoda, like Rav Kook, was tolerant of secular Zionists, but in their case the tolerance derived from universalistic values, not from a religious interpretation of the meaning of secularism. While they would never admit it, it also stemmed, we believe, from their relative indifference to the irreligion of the secular Zionists. As far as the adaptationists were concerned, the attainment of Jewish national goals was no less important than that of religious goals, and their religious objectives (particularly those of *Torah v'avoda*) were directed primarily at combatting the established religious leadership and investing Judaism with nationalist and social meaning rather than at facilitating the return of the secular Zionists to the religious fold. The adaptationists explained Jewish rituals and holidays in nationalist terms (the Sabbath, for example, was perceived as a special day separating Jews from non-Jews and therefore uniting the people, or passages in the Passover liturgy were interpreted as references to national uprisings) and legitimated overtly secular ceremonies (for example, *Torah v'avoda's* interpretation of May Day as a religious festival).

Conclusions

Religious Jews, their leaders in particular, have exhibited a set of attitudes toward Zionism and Israel ranging from intense hostility, on pragmatic and theological grounds, to avid enthusiasm on these same grounds. Viewing the situation from a perspective of over one hundred years, we can make a number of generalizations. The greatest controversy and hostility among religious Jews was generated by Zionist ideology. This ideology has certainly declined in importance. Indeed, as recent Zionist conferences attest, the Zionist movement is in search of an ideology. United Nations resolutions to the contrary, the Zionist movement is not sufficiently alive to arouse the antagonism of anyone familiar with its activity. Zionism has been replaced by Israel as a focus for concern. Rav Zvi Yehuda, as we noted, concerns himself with Israel, not Zionism. Israel is an existing entity, not an idea or an ideology. Antagonism to Israel means hostility to an institution, to a people, and to a state that has been under siege by the enemies of the Jewish people—the object of the most virulent of antisemitic sentiments. Furthermore, because so many religious Jews live in Israel and benefit from the general services it provides, not to mention the special favors it confers on them, they have ample reason to offer Israel their support. Those who are not sympathetic and supportive of Israel tend to be neutral and indifferent rather than antagonistic. With respect to Zionism as an ideology, it is as rare to find a vigorous attack on Zionism in religious circles as it is to find a militant defense of it in nonreligious ones.

Second, within religious Zionist circles, messianic Zionism—either the synthesis of the religious tradition and Zionist ideology offered by Rav Kook or the more extreme formulation of his son—is the dominant ideology. (Its widespread acceptance indicates not that the majority of religious Zionists necessarily embrace it in its pure version, but only that they have no alternative ideology.) We have already suggested why it is natural enough for an ideology that synthesizes Zionism and the religious tradition to attract religious Zionists. We noted the more pragmatic approach of Rav Reines or Rav Amiel, and we could have added the contemporary approach of Yeshayahu Leibowitz, who legitimates the state of Israel by virtue of the desire of Jews to rule themselves but attributes no religious significance whatsoever to it. But, as we said, these approaches are inherently unsatisfactory because they provide no ideological bridge to the general society, and they deny transcendent meaning to the activities in which religious Zionists are engaged. (The latter point is less true of Rav Amiel.) What is remarkable, however, is that no form of ideological synthesis other than that of Rav Kook is alive today. Some of the reasons for this state of affairs and a prognosis of the possible decline of messianic Zionism are to be found in the concluding chapter.

– 6 –

Religious Leaders in the Political Arena

In assessing religious Judaism's approach to Zionism, we referred to a number of approaches. We identified these approaches with rabbinical authorities, almost all of whom were religious rather than political leaders. Nevertheless, their points of view, as we saw, found expression in one or the other of the two major religious parties. Each of these parties also has its leaders, but they are recognized as political rather than religious figures. This designation includes those who are ordained rabbis. The nonreligious public sometimes confuses them, but the religious public usually has little difficulty in distinguishing between their political and religious leaders. In the exceptional cases where there is difficulty, it is generally related to the rise of new religious-political movements. Rabbi Haim Druckman, a leader of Gush Emunim and the head of a yeshiva, is the best recent example.

Political and religious leaders are distinguishable according to three criteria: the qualities necessary for appointment, the means or resources invoked by the leader to enforce his authority, and the nature of his functions.

In the ideal-typical case the religious leader is one whose appointment and authority derive from his religious qualities: piety, knowledge of sacred texts, and in some cases quasi-prophetic or mystical powers. The ideal qualities of the political leader, even the leader of a religious party, are organizational and administrative abilities, daring, ability to sway followers, and decisiveness. The religious leader, even when he has coer-

---

This chapter is an extensive revision of an essay by Eliezer Don-Yehiya, "Religious Leadership and Political Leadership," in *Jewish Spiritual Leadership in Our Time,* ed. Ella Belfer (Jerusalem: Dvir, 1982, in Hebrew), pp. 104–34. An English-language version will appear in *Middle Eastern Studies.*

cive authority, bases his influence primarily on his spiritual qualities. The use of force is less repugnant to a typical political leader. Finally, religious leaders may concern themselves with sociopolitical questions, but they deal primarily in relations between man and God or society and God. When they do involve themselves with sociopolitical questions, their stance is based on their interpretation of sacred scriptures or their understanding of God's commands rather than on their right to decide or their expertise in deciding questions of social policy.

Relations between Religious and Political Leaders in Judaism

Historically the Jewish tradition assumes a division of labor, but an absence of rigid boundaries, between religious and political leaders.[1] Relations between religious and political leaders are a function of relations between religion and state. Judaism's notion of the proper relationship between state and religion stands somewhere between the *organic* and *church* models.[2] According to Donald Smith, the organic model is characterized by the nondifferentiation of religious and political functions. The ruler possesses both spiritual and temporal authority, and his function is to maintain the divine social order. Either there is no independent religious organization, or, if it exists, it is maintained by the ruler. Normative Islam is an example of the organic model. In the church model, governmental and religious institutions are clearly differentiated, regardless of how closely they may cooperate. The religious orientation in the church model is legitimated in its own terms, not in terms of the functions it performs for the social order. The church is in, but not of, society. Relations between the Catholic church and the state in the Catholic countries of Europe were, until recently, classic examples of the church model. Within Judaism, religion is not a distinctive institution, and in this respect it fits the organic model. Jewish religious law concerns itself with social and political matters far more intensely than Christian religious law. But, unlike the organic model of Islam, Judaism doesn't strive for the identification of religious and political leadership. There is overlap in the functions each performs, though each maintains a measure of autonomy. This is the condition that prevailed throughout most of Jewish history, during periods of Jewish political autonomy and throughout most of the Diaspora period, when Jewish communities were subject to outside rule but exercised a fair degree of control over their internal order.

One result of the processes of modernization, secularization, and political emancipation is that relations between religious and political leaders in the Jewish community have increasingly come to resemble the church rather than the organic model. This is true in the Diaspora as well as in contemporary Israel. Political and religious structures and leaders are almost entirely differentiated even within the religious subcommunity. This differentiation stems from developments in the general society from which even the most insulated of religious subgroups is not entirely immune. However, among the ultra-pious, who will not concern us here, these tendencies are less pronounced.

The modern secular state, unlike the traditional one, is built on the assumption that political authority does not need religious legitimation, even in societies where religion and state are not separate. Furthermore, the secular nature of modern society influences relations between religious and political leaders. In the Jewish case, secularization undermined the balance of power that existed between political and religious leaders in traditional Jewish society. In the past, religious leaders relied on the material resources that stood at the disposal of the political leaders in order to assure their own security and buttress their authority. Political leaders relied upon the legitimation of the religious leadership to evoke commitment and loyalty from the members of the community.[3] Secularization resulted in the condition whereby political leaders no longer required the legitimation of religious leaders. However, as we shall see, religious legitimation has assumed renewed importance in Israel in the last two decades.

The development of the new Jewish settlements in the land of Israel, which were relatively free of the constraints and traditions of Diaspora communities, had its own impact on the status of religious leaders for a number of reasons. First, the Zionist immigrants who settled the land, beginning in the 1880s, brought secular conceptions about the autonomous legitimacy of political authority with them. But the settlement also signaled the renewal of Jewish communal authority, which the political emancipation of Jews had undermined. On the one hand, this meant some revival of religious authority. The British mandatory power, for example, was quite anxious that a chief rabbinate be institutionalized and governmental functions be delegated to it. But the revived authority was transmitted by a secular power opening the way to the intervention of political leaders in matters formerly assumed to be the exclusive concern of religious leaders. In fact, the potential for such intervention so troubled some religious leaders that they refused appointment by and official recognition from secular institutions.

Second, Jewish society in the land of Israel, particularly from the period of the second *aliya* (immigrant wave), which came between 1904 and

1914, differed from traditional Jewish society not only in its exclusively secular basis but in its tendency to centralize organization and leadership at the expense of the local community. This tendency was influenced both by ideological currents that the new immigrants brought from the revolutionary movements of Eastern Europe and by the drive for unity and centralization associated with political Zionism from its inception. This orientation strengthened the political leadership vis-à-vis religious leaders, who, functioning in accordance with traditional Jewish patterns, to be described below, tended to resist the centralization of authority. The centralization of political leadership, of course, became even more pronounced following the establishment of the state in 1948.

Third, the renewal of Jewish political sovereignty raised a host of new issues concerning the relationship between the *halakha* and the state. The *halakha*, it was charged, was incapable of resolving questions that arose from conditions of a modern sovereign state. Religious leaders, it was believed, were not interested in or capable of coping with problems whose resolution required radically new religious conceptions. The result, so it was charged, was a widening gap between the reality of a state on the one hand and the *halakha* and its champions on the other. This attitude undermined both the status of religion and of religious leaders.

Fourth, after 1948, masses of traditional Jews deferential to traditional Jewish custom but not punctilious in religious observance came to Israel. Many of them were without political experience or exposure to the influence of secularization. Competition for their allegiance sharpened the conflict between the religious and secular camps in Israel. But it also alerted the secular leaders to the importance of religious institutions and religious symbols in mobilizing the loyalty of these new immigrants. One cannot overstate the impact of this factor on subsequent developments in relations between the secular-political and religious leadership.

Fifth, religion has become an increasingly important component of Israeli political culture. This development is a result of the declining influence of secular Zionist ideologies as sources for symbols and values to legitimate the social order and integrate and mobilize the population. As we emphasized in chapter four, there is growing dependence by the political elite on religious symbols.[4] The modernization process in Judaism and the state of Israel was not associated with a radical secularization of group identity and political culture but rather, at least in the last two decades, with a tendency to reaffirm the religious aspect of a Jewish national identity. The latter identity owes its emergence to modernization and secularization, but, paradoxically, religion and religious symbols have become its source of legitimation.

The effect of these last two developments on the status of religious leaders and their relations with political leaders is inconclusive. On the one hand, it strengthens the authority of religious leaders since even nonreligious circles perceive them as representative of the religious tradition. But the very increase of political influence among religious leaders encourages political leaders (both secular and religious) to interfere in their affairs and seek a voice in their appointment and policies.

TYPES OF RELIGIOUS LEADERS

There are different ways of distinguishing religious leaders, but the single most important distinction in Israel, for purposes of understanding religious-political relations, is the distinction between institutionalized and noninstitutionalized religious leaders. Institutionalized religious leaders owe their authority to the formal position that they hold rather than to their personal qualities. Such leadership has firm roots in Jewish history. But since the tenth century institutionalized religious leaders have functioned primarily at the local, communal level. At the regional or national level Jewish religious leaders owed their authority to their personal qualities, primarily as Torah sages (talmudic authorities).

This situation has changed in Israel. It is no longer true that institutionalized leaders function primarily at the local communal level and Torah sages at the national level. The Chief Rabbinical Council (CRC) is viewed in religious Zionist circles as the supreme religious authority in the state, if not in the world, though its incumbents are not necessarily talmudic luminaries. The CRC is led by Israel's two chief rabbis, one known as the *Ashkenazic* chief rabbi and the other as the *Sephardic* chief rabbi. There are minor differences in Ashkenazic and Sephardic rituals. However, the two are considered chief rabbis of all Israel and not just of those who follow their respective rites. Besides the two chief rabbis, a number of additional rabbis (around ten, though their number varies from time to time) are members of the CRC. The CRC exercises some quasi-governmental and some informal authority over such areas as supervision of meat slaughtering in accordance with Jewish law and other dietary regulations and supervision of religious scribes. They have some responsibility for marriage licenses, confirming rabbinical ordination and similar matters. In addition to presiding over the CRC and carrying out numerous ceremonial functions, the chief rabbis serve as heads of the Supreme Rabbinical Court (the rabbinical court of appeal). The creation of the CRC in 1921 reflects tendencies in the *yishuv* toward institutionalization and centralization. While other factors, to which we will return, led to the formation of the CRC, there was recognition of the need to establish a centralized religious institution to balance the centralized secular leadership.

Opposition to the CRC within the religious community stemmed in part from resistance by the most traditionally religious and generally non-Zionist elements to a centralized religious leadership whose authority derived from office rather than from personal qualities.

Ideological and Sociological Distinctions among Types of Religious Leaders

The institutionalization of the CRC meant legal recognition, funding, transfer of authority from secular political leaders, and the integration of the religious leaders into the secular political system. In addition to the CRC, chief rabbis were appointed to serve local communities. Those religious circles who objected to the establishment of such posts feared the interference of secular elements in rabbinical affairs and efforts to introduce religious reforms. They also objected, in principle, to any cooperation with nonreligious Jews, particularly in matters of religion. There was an additional fear that Zionist leaders would manipulate the CRC to increase Zionist influence in religious life. Religious Jews who refused to recognize the authority of the CRC looked to traditional leaders whose authority derived from their renown as Torah sages or *rebbes* (hasidic leaders believed to possess quasi-mystical qualities and powers). In recent generations even rebbes have not commanded deference unless their followers also deemed them Torah sages.

The differences between institutionalized and noninstitutionalized leaders lie not only in the source of their authority. Members of the CRC are generally practicing rabbis, whereas noninstitutionalized leaders are generally heads of yeshivot or rebbes. In other words, whereas members of the institutionalized rabbinate generally see themselves as the religious leaders of all Jews, religious as well as nonreligious, the Torah sages and rebbes function as authorities to selective groups of very Orthodox Jews.

There is a correlation between type of leader and attitudes toward modernization, Zionism, and the state of Israel. But it is not perfect and one must be careful about hasty dichotomizing. The temptation is to assume that religious leaders whose authority is based on their office have a sense of general societal responsibility and a positive attitude toward modernization, Zionism and the state, and that religious leaders whose authority is based on their personal qualities are responsible only to selective Orthodox groups and are antimodern, anti-Zionist, and indifferent to the existence of a Jewish state. But there are institutionalized religious leaders who are ambivalent in their attitudes toward the state, and rebbes and Torah sages who are among its most ardent supporters. Furthermore, as we have noted, religious ultra-nationalists (Gush Emunim and their sympathizers) have developed their own set of noninstitutionalized leaders in recent years. They are certainly sympathetic to the state, which, together with the land, is at the center of their system of sacred symbols.

The authority of traditional leaders (Torah sages and rebbes) over their followers exceeds the authority of institutionalized leaders over *their* followers. The traditional religious leaders, who focus exclusively on the already committed, certainly have an easier task in imposing their authority. In addition, the very institutionalization of the rabbinate, which entails the involvement of secular authorities in its structure and function, reduces its status in the eyes of its religiously observant constituents.

Religious leaders can protect their authority in secular society in one of two ways. They can stress their autonomy and surrender any claim to government recognition, or they can seek to enhance their authority through government recognition and funding, thereby risking loss of autonomy. Religious leaders who choose the second path may seek the best of both worlds, enhancing their authority through the assistance of secular authorities while struggling to maintain their autonomy, but they are rarely completely successful. Traditional leaders choose the first path; the institutionalized rabbinate choose the second. This course not only strengthens trust in the former's integrity among their own followers but increases their status among some elements within the religious Zionist camp itself. Many religious Zionists accord deference and respect to the CRC or local chief rabbis but view the Torah sages and rebbes as the real models of religious leaders. Furthermore, they accept the decisions of the latter group on questions of Jewish law as authoritative because they are considered the greater experts.

Finally, a good part of the religious public that looks to the institutionalized rabbinate for leadership is more exposed to the influence of modern culture and therefore less likely to accept any type of authority, including religious authority, with blind obedience. This attitude is particularly apparent when religious leaders intervene in matters outside the narrow confines of religion.

The differences between types of leaders and followers are reflected in relations between the political and religious leaders of the two major religious parties in Israel, the National Religious Party (NRP) and Agudat Israel.

Religious Leaders and Political Leaders

The very existence of religious parties is the outcome of secularization and modernization. Indeed, modernization gives rise to all types of political parties, whether secular or religious,[5] as vehicles to engage the masses in the process of governing and to increase their identification with government. In addition, the religious party emerges in defense of the religious public against the forces of secularism and modernization, which threaten its values and style of life. It has also been argued that secularization results in a new type of religio-political leader, who, by virtue of the deference he commands, the authority with which he speaks, and the role he plays in defense of religious interests, becomes something of an alternative to the traditional religious leader.

Donald Smith maintains that the rise of religious parties is associated with the secularization of the religious system, which is reflected in the transfer of the center of religious authority from a priestly elite to a secular elite.[6] One reason for this transfer of authority rests in the increasing importance attributed to the ability to attract and sway masses of followers, which forms the basis of power and political authority and comes at the expense of the sacral qualities of the traditional religious leader. According to Smith, the intellectual, western-educated elite in the developing countries of Asia, Africa, and Latin America considers the traditional religious elite incapable of understanding the kind of adaptation that the modern world demands. Related to this attitude are democratic assumptions that deny the right of any person to speak authoritatively on behalf of an entire society as religious leaders are wont to do. Recent developments—Iran is the most outstanding—suggest caution in viewing religio-political leaders, that is, political leaders of religious parties, as alternatives to religious leaders. The example of Israel suggests that religio-political leaders are a source of support to religious leaders on the one hand but are their competitors and even opponents on the other.

Religio-political leaders rely on the endorsement of religious leaders in their election campaigns. They also look to them to help mobilize support of the religious public in bringing pressure to bear upon secular authorities on behalf of religious interests. Religious leaders, in turn, rely on party leaders to defend them and their institutions from secular interference and control. But, despite the common goals and mutual dependence of religio-political and religious leaders, they differ in many respects.

The conflicts between them reflect differences over the way they relate to political life. Like all political leaders, religious party leaders must take into account considerations of political reality. Since they are directly involved in political conflicts over power and influence and seek to influence secular leaders and even voters, they tend toward flexibility and accommodation. In contrast, religious leaders are less involved in conflicts over power and influence in the political system.

By virtue of their intense and prolonged socialization within the strictest confines of the religious world, the significant reference groups for religious leaders are different from those of the political elite, and their perception of reality is also quite different. Rabbis do not seek political office. They do not have to satisfy or answer to an electorate or political figures. They seek the recognition and approval of their religious peers and religious mentors—preeminently of other talmudic scholars. Their code of right and wrong is dictated by their own religious understanding, their own perception of Jewish history and Jewish law, their own sense of the needs of the hour, and the internal pressures to which they are subject from within the religious world. Since they cannot conceive of themselves as living outside that world (nor could they remain religious leaders if they did), the kinds of political and even material rewards and sanctions that political leaders can offer them seem to them ephemeral. Finally, they believe they are spokesmen for divine authority. Pragmatic considerations necessarily play a smaller role to those with such a world view.

The approach of religious leaders to public religious issues is, therefore, more rigid and less compromising than that of religio-political leaders. This difference is a source of tension, which is likely to increase when one encroaches on the other's sphere. The party leaders' need for legitimation emboldens religious leaders to interfere in their affairs and to offer active guidance on the political level. This interference, among other factors, induces party leaders to try to influence the composition and policy of the ecclesiastical leadership in order to bring it into line with its own policies and interests—an attempt that leads to additional competition and tensions between the two sets of leaders.

Which of the two sides is more influential? It is instructive to compare Catholic church and Jewish religious leaders. The church exercises enormous influence, if not actual control, over most Catholic institutions and services, Catholic schools in particular. When religious-political parties were founded in predominantly Catholic countries, the church did not always welcome them but exercised influence over them. The church has lost much of that influence in the last two decades. On the other hand, it still retains a voice within the parties and complete autonomy over its own affairs with respect to the religious parties.

In Israel, religious parties developed before an institutionalized religious leadership. Indeed, the religious institutions themselves were, to a great extent, created through the initiative of religious parties. Even Agudat Israel's Council of Torah Sages was created as a formalized institution by the party. Furthermore, as we have seen, the two major religious school systems in Israel were founded, directed, and protected by the religious parties. This involvement afforded them a role in the socialization of religious youth and strengthened their image as patrons of religious interests.

The similarities between the NRP and Agudat Israel must not be overstated. We will look first at the measure of CRC intervention in NRP affairs and then at NRP intervention in the CRC. Then we turn to Agudat Israel and its relations with the Council of Torah Sages. Finally, we will compare these relations with those between the church and the religious parties in Catholic countries.

One reason religious Zionists established the CRC was because the rebbes and heads of yeshivot who were acknowledged as the outstanding talmudic authorities were opposed to Zionism and the religious Zionist movement. The religious Zionists needed legitimation, which they could not get from traditional religious authorities, and therefore sought a new type of religious leader who would grant them that legitimacy. The NRP seeks to strengthen the CRC's influence in secular society. They declare their loyalty to the CRC and acceptance of its authority on public issues, but they also seek to influence its composition and policies to accord with party interests.

There have been a few issues on which the CRC's stand has had a major influence on NRP policy. In practice, NRP readiness to accept the authority of the chief rabbis on political subjects is selective and depends on the degree of congruence between the position of the party and the rabbis, the relative strength of these bodies at the particular time, and the degree of public support for the position in question. Thus, in this respect, rabbinical influence over the NRP varies according to the degree of internal unity or conflict within and between party and religious leaders. But in theory the NRP recognizes the religious leaders' right to intervene, at least to a certain degree, in their decisions and activities. Religious parties in Israel differ from most religious parties in Europe or Latin America in this respect. The NRP has shown greater acceptance of rabbinical intervention than Christian Democratic parties are wont to allow the church.

On the other hand, the NRP's role in protecting the CRC has contributed to its feeling that it can act in the role of patron. The party has had considerable influence over the choice of the CRC and local chief rabbis, but its influence over their policies is far from decisive.[7] Some chief rabbis have been chosen over NRP opposition, and others who owe their appointment to the NRP nevertheless maintain their independence. As we shall see, the NRP has recently been constrained to delay elections to the CRC because of its dissatisfaction with the composition of the electing body. The fact that a majority of that body has traditionally consisted of rabbis and judges of rabbinical courts indicates how limited NRP control actually is over the Israeli rabbinate. Many rabbis, including those who serve in institutionalized religious positions, received their training in yeshivot led by Torah sages and are more sympathetic to Agudat Israel and its policies than to the NRP.

Agudat Israel, in turn, accepts without reservation the authority of the Council of Torah Sages on all subjects; not only on halakhic topics or issues of general policy but even on questions of political tactics and strategy, should the council so choose to express itself. The authority of the Council of Torah Sages, on the other hand, does not flow from the formal position of this institution but from the personal authority of its members, who are recognized by the community identified with Agudat Israel as the final arbiters and experts in *halakha*. In establishing the Council of Torah Sages, Agudat Israel did not establish a new kind of religious authority; rather it expressed its readiness to accept the rule of traditional religious leaders and established a formal framework within which they might function. More than the council needs the party, the party needs *it* in order to legitimize itself and gain the support of those circles which unequivocally demur to traditional religious authority. Hence, interference by Agudat Israel's political leaders in council affairs would be most illegitimate.

The differences between the Council of Torah Sages and the CRC are reflected not only in the selection of members to these bodies but in their structure and functions. From time to time, members of the Council of Torah Sages decide among themselves to add new members. The members of the CRC are selected for a fixed period, in accordance with established regulations. The CRC also has clearly defined powers and jurisdiction in specific halakhic areas. The Council of Torah Sages has no defined powers or functions: it has no administrative staff, nor does it operate according to strict procedures. The members meet at the request of Agudat Israel leaders or at their own initiative when the need arises to instruct the party about decisions on contemporary political issues.

In summary, there is much less of a tendency toward autonomy and mutual nonintervention between religious and religio-political leaders in Israel than in Catholic countries. When Christian Democratic parties were first established, the principle of separating political and religious authority was invoked to justify demands for autonomy by Christian Democratic party and professional association leaders.[8] The nature of traditional Judaism, discussed above, and its central role within the history and culture of the Jewish people are among the factors that make any rigid delineation of boundaries between religious and religio-political leaders virtually impossible.

In comparing relationships between the CRC and NRP with those of the Catholic church and Christian Democratic parties, we find that the church is more influential than the CRC. No Christian Democratic party would dare inject itself into church affairs the way the NRP injects itself into CRC affairs. On the other hand, comparing relationships between the Council of Torah Sages and Agudat Israel with those prevailing between the church and religio-political parties in Catholic countries, we find that the Council of Torah Sages is more influential than the church. The church would not dare inject itself into or so blatantly seek to instruct Christian Democratic parties as the Council of Torah Sages does with Agudat Israel.

We now turn our attention to relations between religious leaders and secular political leaders. We will first inquire about the extent to which religious leaders intervene in Israeli political life, a topic that will necessarily involve a discussion of pressures on the religious leaders themselves. We will then look more specifically at the efforts of political leaders to intervene in the affairs of religious leaders. We will focus most of our attention on the CRC, which, because of its institutional, quasi-governmental character, is more directly and continually involved in general political life.

The CRC in the Political Arena

CRC involvement in political life has been a function not only of its institutional base of support but of the personalities and proclivities of the chief rabbis who lead the institution. The first chief rabbis, Rav Kook and Rav Meir (Ashkenazic and Sephardic, respectively), who were selected in 1921, sought to preserve the independence of their office and to rely on the widest possible support in religious circles, including that of those who refused to recognize the authority and legitimacy of the political institutions of the *yishuv*. This explains why the chief rabbis resisted the integration of their office into the formal network of institutions of the *yishuv*. Such integration was anticipated by the British mandatory statute that defined the office and status of the chief rabbis and the CRC. As a consequence, the CRC received no funds from the institutions of the *yishuv,* and this hampered its work. Rav Kook, in particular, undertook the rather impossible effort of placating everybody in order to gain acceptance from all segments of the Jewish population. He never gained the acceptance he strove for, but his own activities were paralyzed as a result of his futile efforts.[9]

The second set of chief rabbis, Herzog (elected in 1936) and Ouziel (elected in 1939), integrated their office into the institutions of the *yishuv* and, later on, those of the state. They were also more active in general political life than were their predecessors. They involved themselves in areas of public policy concerning Jewish rights to the land of Israel and the political status of the Jewish state. This activity was not in opposition to the policies of the secular leadership but supplementary to them. Even when undertaken independently, it was in line with those policies on which there was broad consensus within the *yishuv* or the state.

Both Herzog and Ouziel were ardent Zionists, and they perceived Israel's establishment as pointing to divine Redemption. Nevertheless, both of them, Herzog in particular, sought to create a united religious camp and to attract the support of non-Zionist religious circles to the chief rabbinate. These efforts were an important part of the decision by all the religious parties (there were four of them at the time) to enter a joint slate in the elections to the First Knesset and to maintain a single parliamentary block, the United Religious Front.

In the early years of statehood, the basic political arrangements in the sphere of religious affairs were negotiated between Mapai and the religious parties. The chief rabbis played an active role through their influence over the policies of the religious parties. This intervention evoked criticism from political leaders, both secular and religious. Nevertheless, secular authorities turned to the chief rabbis, Herzog in particular, to use their influence to quiet the opposition of religious circles abroad to certain policies of the state. For example, in the controversy over whether women were to be drafted into the Israeli army and under what conditions religious women were to be exempt, negotiations apparently took place directly between the then prime minister, Moshe Sharett, and Chief Rabbi Herzog. There were those who denied, on principle, the rabbis' right to involve themselves in political matters. Ben Gurion felt particularly strongly about this issue, and it may be more than coincidence that negotiations between the prime minister and the chief rabbi took place when he temporarily resigned from office. Secular political leaders were particularly vexed by the chief rabbis' electoral support for the religious parties, support that was more readily rendered in view of the formation of the United Religious Front.

The CRC was weakened by the death of Rav Ouziel in 1954 and the extended illness of Rav Herzog, who died in 1959. In 1955 Rav Nissim was elected to succeed Ouziel as Sephardic chief rabbi, and he functioned, in fact, as the sole chief rabbi until the election of Rav Unterman as Ashkenazic chief rabbi in 1963.

Nissim's style was one of confrontation. He refused to participate in a memorial service for Israel's first president because the ceremonial was not in accordance with the religious tradition and was fixed according to the secular rather than the Hebrew date of his death. He refused to participate in ceremonies welcoming the Pope when the latter visited Israel. The CRC under Nissim's leadership engaged in controversies over a number of political-religious issues. Among the most widely publicized was that involving the Jewish status of the B'nei Israel, a small Indian Jewish sect whose members had immigrated to Israel. Nissim refused at first to recognize them as Jews. To most Israelis this decision appeared callous and in conflict with the Zionist vision of "ingathering the exiles from the four corners of the earth."

Mapai's dissatisfaction with Nissim led to an additional controversy over elections to the CRC, scheduled for 1960. In anticipation of the elections, an effort was made to replace Nissim with Ovadia Yosef and to elect Shlomo Goren as Ashkenazic chief rabbi. This effort was connected to Mapai's strategy of weakening NRP influence over religious affairs, a strategy developed when the NRP resigned from the government over the "Who is a Jew?" issue in 1958. Mapai was assisted by Rabbi Moshe Toledano, minister of religious affairs, an opponent of both the NRP and Chief Rabbi Nissim, against whom he had contested the 1955 elections for Sephardic chief rabbi.

Toledano's authority to establish procedures for the election of the CRC was fully exploited in order to disqualify nominees who might compete with Ovadia Yosef and Goren. However, the CRC and NRP, with the cooperation of other parties, succeeded in postponing the elections. When they finally took place three years later, Nissim was reelected as Sephardic chief rabbi, and Isser Unterman, the NRP candidate, succeeded in overcoming Goren for the post of Ashkenazic chief rabbi by a few votes.

In the Unterman-Nissim period (1963–71), the two chief rabbis clashed with one another. This undermined the CRC's capacity to function. In addition, the chief rabbis' involvement in a number of political-religious issues, the most important of which were the 1969 "Who is a Jew?" question and problems of personal status, brought them into sharp dispute with secular authorities. Demands grew to find a permanent solution to the problem of Jews ineligible to marry partners of their choice in accordance with *halakha*. They were helpless because, as we noted in chapter two, according to Israeli law, Jews could only marry (or divorce) in accordance with *halakha*. Pressures arose to induce the rabbis either to accommodate themselves to public conceptions of morality or to legislate civil marriage. Tensions and pressures reached their peak in the case of the *mamzerim* (sing: *mamzer;* a child of an illicit union, as defined by Jewish law, who is ineligible to marry anyone but a convert to Judaism or another *mamzer*). The most celebrated case involved a brother and sister who both became engaged while serving in the Israeli army. The latter point is important because, while on active duty in the army, an Israeli enjoys something approaching sacred status in the popular mind. Nothing is, ostensibly, too good for a soldier of the Israeli Defense Forces. In this case the rabbinate was denying them the right to marry partners to whom they were engaged because, it was suddenly discovered, they were, unbeknownst to themselves, *mamzerim*. NRP leaders were most uncomfortable with the CRC's stance, since they feared that rabbinical intransigence could undermine the whole set of arrangements that had been reached with secular parties granting rabbis control over the area of personal status. This case was one of the reasons that led the NRP to support the candidacy of Goren in his second try for the post of Ashkenazic chief against the incumbent Unterman. As a result of an NRP–Labor Party agreement (the Labor Party was Mapai's successor party), and despite overwhelming support for Unterman among rabbis and rabbinical court judges who constituted the electoral assembly, Goren was elected chief rabbi along with Ovadia Yosef, who defeated Nissim.

Shortly after his election, Goren made good on the promise implicit in his election and found a halakhic loophole to declare the brother and sister, previously defined as *mamzerim,* eligible to marry the partners of their choice. This action was vigorously denounced by Agudat Israel circles. They maintained that Goren's ruling was in violation of *halakha,* as it indeed appeared to be to most observers. Ovadia Yosef, in a more restrained manner, also suggested as much. These circles, which included the majority of leading rabbinical figures—certainly most of the heads of the talmudic academies—had long had reservations about Goren's integrity.[10] Their condemnation may also have been influenced by his messianic ideology—the conception that the establishment of the state of Israel points to the imminent realization of Judaism's messianic vision. Some of his enemies charged that Goren's hubris in his halakhic decisions and personal conduct suggested that he believed himself to be the messiah.

The conflicts between Goren and his opponents led to pronounced changes in relations between the CRC and the noninstitutionalized religious leaders represented by the rebbes, Torah sages, and their constituents. Goren's predecessors as chief rabbis sought their approval and support. In fact, this search for approval from the ultra-orthodox led to a certain indecisiveness and lack of consistency in CRC policy, which avoided clear-cut decisions in some cases for fear of evoking criticism from noninstitutionalized religious leaders. On the other hand, while the Torah sages never recognized the CRC as supreme religious leaders, they avoided open hostility and sometimes cooperated on an ad hoc basis.

Following Goren's election these circles sought to delegitimate the Ashkenazic chief rabbi and his followers. This sharpened the division within the religious public and heightened the conflict between the two chief rabbis and their followers, since Ovadia Yosef maintained cordial relations with Goren's opponents. (The rabbis came to an understanding during the last few years of their tenure.)

The two chief rabbis were also divided by fundamental ideological orientations. Ovadia Yosef never accepted Goren's messianic theology. Their differences were reflected in disputes over what blessings should or should not be recited on Independence Day and over such broad policy issues as whether Jewish law prohibits Israel from relinquishing territory captured in the Six-Day War. Much has been written of Gush Emunim and its messianic theology, which Goren also expresses. It should be noted that many Israeli rabbis within the religious Zionist camp, not to mention virtually everyone outside it, do not accept a messianic theology. But they have generally been silent on this point since the Six-Day War. On the other hand, the two chief rabbis elected in 1983, Abraham Shapiro and Mordecai Eliyahu, are both advocates of a messianic theology and are part of Merkaz Harav circles.

Political Intervention of Secular Authorities in Affairs of Religious Leaders

Our previous discussion indicated how the chief rabbis' stance in public affairs invited the intervention of political leaders in their selection. It is useful, however, to review the story from a more theoretical perspective.

The Torah sages and rebbes who lead Agudat Israel have eschewed recognition and support of governmental authorities. They, in turn, have retained complete independence. They have sought to influence general social policy, especially in recent years. Although one would anticipate that political involvement in the general society would expose religious leaders to reciprocal political pressure, traditional religious leaders have successfully resisted those pressures that have been exerted. This is less true of the institutionalized religious leaders. Smith has observed that the expansion of the political system to areas that were heretofore part of the religious system is one characteristic of the secularization of the political system. A second characteristic is the separation of the political system from religious ideologies and ecclesiastical structures. A third characteristic, which will not concern us, is the transvaluation of the political culture to incorporate secular political values.[11]

Separation of the political and religious systems implies the contraction of a government's authority to act in matters considered the province of religious leaders. Expansion implies the opposite. However, both separation and expansion can occur simultaneously and may be related. The state, for example, may refrain from supporting religious institutions and also expand its activity to areas in which religious institutions have exercised authority. But nonseparation of the religious leadership from the political system is certainly compatible with the expansion of governmental functions at the expense of religious authorities. Indeed, nonseparation, as the Israeli case exemplifies, may strengthen the process of expansion.

This expansion of the secular political system into religious areas is not only a matter of increased governmental responsibility in fields such as education or health or welfare, which were once the responsibility of religious leaders. It is also reflected in the efforts of some political leaders to intervene in matters which, by any definition, are the province of religious leaders. The method is to influence the composition of the religious leadership and exert pressures on religious leaders to adapt their policies to those of the political leaders. Nonseparation of religion and state provides opportunity and legitimation for such pressure, but other factors provide the incentive. There are three basic incentives that have led Israeli political leaders to intervene in religious affairs: principle, public policy, and self-interest.

Principle

Many political leaders believe that the modern state is responsible for all important activity affecting the public, including cultural affairs. In Israel, this point of view was expressed most forcefully by David Ben

Gurion and his followers in the ideology of Statism.[12] Ben Gurion maintained that the state and its institutions were the primary focus of citizen loyalty and identification and the absolute source of law and authority. Statism sought to expand the activity and authority of the state and its leaders and to transfer to them functions heretofore performed by parties, interest groups, and even religious institutions. Statists were also resentful of the religious leaders' claim to the allegiance of the religious population, which was based on the notion that religious authority derived from a transcendent and ultimate source, not from the state.

Statists were prepared to offer state recognition and funding to religious institutions and to confer governmental authority upon them in matters such as marriage and divorce. But Ben Gurion and his followers stressed that this willingness must not be interpreted as recognition of the sovereign authority of religious law or of the independent status of religious institutions who interpret and execute the law. Ben Gurion's repeated declaration that Israel is governed by law and not *halakha* was intended to remove any vestige of doubt that the coercive authority of religious laws and institutions derived from the powers of the state, and that the state alone would determine the scope of religious law and the manner in which it was to be implemented.[13]

Ben Gurion also sought to limit the influence of religious leaders in political life (for example, communal rabbis are not eligible to run in Knesset elections) and to subject religious institutions to the control of the state. A number of Israeli Supreme Court decisions have reiterated that rabbinical courts and the rabbinate are subject to state law. On one occasion the Supreme Court ordered the CRC to desist from a particular act. Religious leaders have resisted this aspect of Statism. Tensions over questions of sovereignty are less acute today than in the past; they have generally been resolved in the direction dictated by the statists. But the government has also learned that there are limits to the control they can exercise, given the vigorous support that religious leaders can anticipate from religio-political leaders and religious Jews in general, in defense of their autonomy.

Policy

Political leaders sometimes intervene in religious affairs because of their sense that the policies and activities of religious leaders are politically relevant and can influence the public and the party system. This feeling stems from the importance that religious and even nonreligious voters (particularly those who define themselves as traditional) attribute to the stance of religious leaders.

The efforts to influence religious leaders take the forms of persuasion, direct pressure, and interference in the selection of religious leaders. As we have seen, the attempt is made to elect candidates most favorable to the stance of secular authorities or most amenable to pressure. We will return to this point in our case study of the selection of the chief rabbis.

Self-Interest

As we indicated, the religious leaders are influential figures among part of the Israeli electorate. Therefore parties, factions within parties, individual leaders, and interest groups seek their endorsement. In addition, religious institutions are a source of political power because the religious services they provide create relations of dependency with a portion of the public.

We noted above that the mass immigration following the establishment of the state brought hundreds of thousands of more or less religiously observant Jews, especially from Moslem countries. The nonreligious parties—Mapai, the dominant labor party, in particular—were unwilling to waive their support. Hence they involved themselves in areas they had once recognized as the exclusive province of the religious parties: for example, they appointed a Minister of Religious Affairs sympathetic to them rather than to the NRP, they organized religious schools under their auspices, and they sought to organize synagogue officials in an organization from which they expected political support.

In the conflict between Mapai and the NRP (or its predecessor party) an understanding was achieved over candidates and selection procedures for the CRC, local chief rabbis, and local religious councils and over the distribution of religious services. Following the Likud's 1977 election victory, their representatives were added to the interparty negotiations over the selection of religious officials. Agudat Israel was not invited to participate in these arrangements. Nevertheless, it exercised an influence, since, as we noted, so many rabbis felt closer to it than to the NRP and were willing to follow its signals about preferred candidates.

The most recent elections to the CRC were postponed a number of times and finally scheduled for 1978. Shaul Yisraeli was proposed as the candidate to succeed Goren. Although Yisraeli was a religious Zionist, he was supported by circles sympathetic to Agudat Israel, by most rabbis and rabbinical court judges, and by Ovadia Yosef and his followers. Goren, on the other hand, was supported by a majority of the NRP, the Labor Party, and the Likud. The political parties realized that, given the composition of the electoral body that selects the CRC, Goren's reelection was not assured. Hence, despite the fact that all the legal arrangements had been concluded, the Knesset hurriedly adopted a special law canceling the elections.

The cancellation was rationalized by the need for time to enable the government to prepare a new law defining the duties and composition of the CRC and changing the manner of election to it. In 1980 the Knesset passed such a law, which was intended to eliminate or at least reduce the conflict between the two chief rabbis, a source of embarrassment to everybody. Before the new law was enacted, both chief rabbis served as heads of the CRC and chairmen of the Rabbinical Supreme Court simultaneously. This joint appointment, it was believed, contributed to the friction between them, and when the friction became unmanageable, the result was paralysis of both the CRC and the Rabbinical Supreme Court. According to the new law, one chief rabbi is to serve as head of the CRC and the other as chairman of the Rabbinical Supreme Court during the first half of their terms. They are to rotate their posts during the second half of their terms. The CRC's term of office remained five years, but the chief rabbis' terms were extended to ten years, with incumbents disqualified for immediate reelection. Elections were finally held in 1983, and two new chief rabbis were chosen after a government proposal to amend the act and permit reelection of the incumbents was narrowly defeated by the Knesset.

Important changes were also made in the manner of elections to the CRC. It was enlarged to twenty members: the two chief rabbis, the two chief rabbis of each of Israel's four largest cities, and ten additional rabbis, to be elected by an electoral assembly. The assembly's composition, as in the past, was to include eighty rabbis and seventy public representatives. The law introduced one important change. Members of the assembly are no longer elected, as they were in the past, by bodies composed primarily of religious figures. They are to be selected in accordance with fixed procedures that give a decisive advantage to the parties.

The new law may reduce the politicization of the CRC by establishing procedures for selection of its members in statutory law. The limitation of the chief rabbis to one ten-year term without the right to immediate reelection will reduce the influence of external political pressures on the chief rabbis once they have been elected. But the law may increase politicization because it strengthens partisan influence on the composition of the electoral assembly. Most of its members are appointed by political leaders or identified with political governmental bodies such as local governments or local religious councils. The minister of religious affairs' right to nominate 20 of the 150 assembly members provides him with wide influence, especially since he also appoints the chairman of the election committee to supervise the administrative side of organizing the election. The new law reduces the number of rabbinical court judges in the assembly to ten. Thus, those whose authority as talmudic experts is most widely recognized have the least influence in the selection of the CRC.

Conclusion

Those who warn that nonseparation of religion and state corrupts the religious establishment can point to the office of the chief rabbinate in confirmation. There is no question that nonseparation has politicized the selection of chief rabbis. Less explicable, however, is why the very standards, rules, and regulations governing the selection of chief rabbis should have become subjects of political manipulation when Israeli politicians would not dream of treating the rules by which a president, or judges, or even Knesset members are elected in so cavalier a manner. The answer, we suspect, rests in the fact that the NRP, which has always loomed as the special guardian of the chief rabbinate, has taken the lead in seeking to manipulate the laws by which the chief rabbis are selected. Paradoxically, they have used their own status to delegitimate or desacralize the rules governing the election. Other parties have only followed in their wake. The willingness and capacity of the NRP to act in such a manner stems, in turn, from the nontraditionalism of the procedures—from the modern implications in the very election of a chief rabbi.

But having observed the corruption of the procedures, we find that it is no less significant that once elected, chief rabbis have acted independently of their political patrons. Goren's early decisions as chief rabbi were very much the exception to this rule. We hold no brief for the office of chief rabbi. We favor abolishing it. But we doubt if this would affect religion or state very much, except, perhaps, to slightly raise the dignity of the religious establishment.

– 7 –

The Anatomy of a Religious Party

The previous chapter explored the relationships between religious and political leaders. In this chapter we focus on the relationships between the leaders of the religious parties and their constituents. We confine our attention to the National Religious Party (NRP) rather than Agudat Israel because the options for both political leaders and followers are more limited in the latter party. In addition, the NRP has recently undergone a radical decline in electoral strength. Exploring this decline will contribute to our understanding of the particular nature of a religious-political party.

From its establishment in 1956 until 1981 the NRP was more stable than any secular party in three respects. First, no group within the NRP ever seceded. Second, its constituents shared the party's commitment to the general principles of religious Zionism, seeking to protect and expand the influence of religion in Israeli society out of a belief that the establishment of Israel was an act of religious significance. Third, its representation in nine Knesset elections never fell below ten seats or exceeded twelve.

The structural, ideological, and electoral stability of the NRP (some of which endured after 1981) was shared by Agudat Israel (the other major religious party, which, unlike the NRP, saw no religious significance to the establishment of Israel). This does not mean that conflict has not occurred within religious parties. In fact, we will argue, certain structural features of the NRP encouraged conflict while safeguarding basic party solidarity.

This chapter is based on an article in Hebrew by Eliezer Don-Yehiya, which appeared in *Medina V'memshal*, no. 14 (1980).

The Anatomy of a Religious Party

The stability of the NRP and the recent changes it has undergone are best understood by examining what has been called the "youth revolution" in its ranks. Generational conflicts have divided other parties, but in those cases the veterans either defeated the young challengers or coopted them. The general pattern was to elevate a few younger leaders who were faithful to one or another veteran leader. The NRP was the only party in which the young attained commanding positions as an independent and united faction in opposition to the party elite. The Young Faction's success took place without splitting the party. But this success, as we shall see, bore within it the seeds of the party's decline, although it is still too early to predict if this decline is temporary or permanent.

The NRP's organizational, ideological, and electoral stability in the past is best explained by its existence as a camp-party. A camp-party represents a subgroup (camp) within the society distinguished by its unique values and behavioral patterns. The members of the camp are integrated into a system of institutions and organizations that extend to all spheres of life. They are linked to a political party by a network of economic, social, and ideological relationships.

The NRP's Structured Factionalism

The fact that the NRP is a camp-party explains its most significant organizational feature, structured factionalism. Structured factionalism refers to the existence of recognized factions within the party that provide the vehicle for elevation to party leadership. Agudat Israel, which represents a second religious camp, is also organized in structured factions. This feature distinguishes both religious parties from the secular ones.

In a system of structured factionalism the party's central committee is composed of factional representatives whose numbers are proportionate to their relative weight within the party. The factions may retain the right to publicize their views independently of the central party organs. Each faction may even sustain its own social, educational, and economic institutions, which integrate its members and solidify their stance behind the faction. In an extreme case, the party becomes a kind of federation or coalition of subparties, with the central party organs functioning only to coordinate the factions' political activities.[1]

Structured factionalism characterizes political parties in Japan and Italy. In Israel, factional differences have been institutionalized in some secular parties. But the factions have generally either been neutralized by the dominant leaders or have become the forerunners of splinter groups that eventually seceded from the party. In contrast, religious party factions, whether in the NRP or Agudat Israel, have remained faithful to the principle of party unity because they are part of camp-parties, because they see themselves as constituting one part of a bloc of constituents who share far more in common with one another than with any other group in the society and who must stand together to protect the interests that they share with one another. In fact, religious party factions have been vehicles for maintaining party loyalty by socializing their supporters to the values of the camp. Hence, among the religious parties, the faction was never conceived of as an entity separate from or demanding a higher loyalty than the party itself, much less the party's constituency.

In the NRP, in particular, competition between the factions enables NRP members to express their discontent with the party leaders or policies in internal elections. Party members become arbiters among elites who lead the NRP factions. Within the camp of religious Zionists, the NRP factions serve the very functions that political parties perform in the general society. A camp-party requires such factions because its supporters are not quite free to transfer their support to other parties in the way that other voters are free. Hence, the only real sanction that the member of a camp has over his party is through the system of structured factionalism. The rise of the Youth Faction, which organized itself around a socially distinctive group and eventually evolved a distinctive ideology, unintentionally eroded the very principles that had maintained NRP unity and stability. Party and even camp loyalty become secondary to ideology, and the seeds of the NRP decline were planted.

The Rise of the Youth Faction in the NRP

The Youth Faction was established in the 1960s as a result of resentment on the part of younger NRP members against the reluctance of the veteran leaders to hold elections to a party convention. From the time of its establishment in 1963 until the mid-1970s, the Youth Faction campaigned under the banner of party democracy and against the oligarchic tendencies of the older leaders.

A change in attitude occurred when the Youth Faction discovered that, through agreements with other factions, it could obtain a large share of influence without competing for the support of the party's rank and file. Its greatest victory was achieved through a secret agreement with leaders of a rival faction to overthrow that faction's leader, Yitzhak Raphael, the party's "strong man" and the Youth Faction's bitterest enemy within the party. In the resulting reallocation of power, the Youth Faction emerged as the strongest, or at least one of the two strongest, factions. In order to avoid internal elections, the Youth Faction subsequently joined the other major factions in a single slate of candidates to the party convention, which reflected the relative weight of each faction. But despite the apparent show of unity, the continued attacks of the Youth Faction on the older leadership not only weakened the leadership's legitimacy among religious voters but multiplied rivalries among the party elite, who were anxious to avoid the Youth Faction's castigations. Deference to the Youth Faction stemmed from the status of their leaders and followers, to which we will return. At this point we note only that the attacks that the Youth Faction leveled against the party leadership not only served to weaken that leadership but contributed to a general loss of the party's status in the minds of religious Zionist voters. When the Youth Faction, having achieved a position of influence within the party, became a partner to the cancellation of internal elections, it only heightened the cynicism of many NRP supporters toward their party and may have eased their subsequent break with the party.

THE YOUTH FACTION: ITS ORIGINS AND SOCIAL BACKGROUND

The NRP Youth Faction had a number of natural advantages that contributed to its rapid development. The age of its members, most of whom were in their twenties at the time of its formation, was only one factor contributing to its sense of solidarity. The faction was composed primarily of the party's young intelligentsia: professionals and managers rather than manual laborers, native-born Israelis of European (Ashkenazic) rather than Asian or north African (Sephardic) origin.[2] Youth Faction members were socialized in the network of institutions associated with the religious Zionist camp, which further reinforced their sense of unity. For example, they attended the same type of elementary and often the same secondary school, met each other in the religious Zionist youth movement, served together in the army or at least underwent a similar army experience, and, in many instances, attended Bar-Ilan University. The Youth Faction built on this sense of solidarity. In addition, many

Youth Faction leaders gained political experience and some degree of recognition, at least among their peers, through service as youth movement leaders and as NRP appointees in the framework of the party's Young Guard. This division of the party had been organized in order to provide some representation to and elicit support from the younger generation of religious Zionists. It was comparable, in many respects, to a women's division. But the younger generation did not feel they were adequately represented among party leaders, and this strengthened the Youth Faction's appeal. Data on the social characterization of the NRP leadership in the early 1960s confirm that the party elite was composed of professional politicians of Eastern European extraction who obtained their posts before, or immediately following, the establishment of the state. This group resisted the inclusion of new forces in its midst and provided a convenient rallying cry for the Youth Faction, who demanded the renewal and rejuvenation of the leadership and a reassessment of its decision-making processes.

Young people in other Israeli parties were also frustrated by their exclusion from positions of power, particularly before the early 1970s. Political life was dominated by the generation of pioneers who came to Israel in the 1920s and 1930s and were now in their sixties, seventies, and eighties. But the problem in the NRP was especially severe. In a party organized along factional lines, the principle of factional representation makes it particularly difficult to provide appropriate representation to natural groups (those based on age, sex, class, origin, etc.), since such groupings do not ordinarily serve as a legitimate basis for factional organization.

In 1972 the Youth Faction won about 20 percent of the vote in party elections, in competition with four other factions. The size of its vote induced other factions to appoint young people to leadership positions. In other words, as a result of the Youth Faction's growth, its own influence increased, and the influence of young people in other factions increased as well. The increased presence of young people in leadership positions had ideological implications, as we shall see. Another result of the Youth Faction vote was to increase the representation of Sephardic Jews in the NRP leadership. Sephardic Jews, who represented about half of all NRP voters, were grossly underrepresented in the central party organs.[3] Although they did not organize as an independent faction, other NRP groups increased their efforts to enlist them into their ranks as a counterweight to the Youth Faction. In fact, however, such appointees generally lacked influence and Sephardic frustration grew unabated until it exploded in 1981.

IDEOLOGICAL CHANGES IN THE NRP

"Change and Renewal," the slogan of the Youth Faction, was directed not only at the party leadership but at its policies as well. Paradoxically, the Youth Faction's criticism was directed at the gap between the party principles to which the Israeli-born religious Zionist youth had been socialized and the willingness of party leaders to compromise those principles in the national political arena. Compromise and concession are foregone conclusions to professional politicians. Educators and youth leaders attach greater importance to consistency and maintenance of principle. Youth leaders, in particular, free from the constraints and temptations of the political world, tend to ignore the gap between the desirable and the possible and convey to their charges their contempt for politicians. This is particularly true in a religious party, where virtually everything the party stands for is legitimated in religious terms, thereby implying that it is nonnegotiable.

The Youth Faction began by emphasizing its loyalty to religion and morality, thereby leveling criticism, indirect if not direct, at the party leadership, whose characteristic stance was one of compromise. A second basic plank in the Youth Faction platform was its insistence that the NRP extend its concerns beyond the protection of religious interests. This conception, which more than any other was destined to undermine the NRP's stability, reflects the perceptions of Israeli-born religious youth.

Israeli-born religious Zionists, middle-class Ashkenazim in particular, were involved in, and felt themselves a part of, general Israeli culture and society. Unlike many of their immigrant parents, who brought the religious culture of Eastern Europe with them and never felt comfortable in Israeli society, the younger generation sought to acquire status and influence in Israeli society and culture. They were unhappy that the NRP confined itself to narrow religious interests (such as maintaining Sabbath rest laws or kashrut standards), assuming a policeman's role in these areas. They were dissatisfied with the classic NRP policy of reaching an accommodation with the secular parties by conceding to the latter's demands on general social and political issues in return for concessions on religious issues—a policy that evoked widespread disdain in the general public. In fact, the Youth Faction's critique tended to take past NRP achievements in the protection of religious interests for granted and sought to look beyond them.

Following the Six-Day War the demand to engage in a political struggle over general social issues focused increasingly on establishing Jewish settlements on the West Bank and maintaining Jewish rule over these territories. The Youth Faction was not the only element within the NRP to oppose Israeli withdrawal from the territories or to favor Jewish settlements, but they became this issue's major standard-bearer within the party. They succeeded thereby in attracting other party members of a hawkish orientation. In fact, at the time of the Yom Kippur War, a transfactional group, Emunim, committed to Jewish settlement of the territories, was organized within the party. When the group decided to base itself outside the NRP framework, under the name Gush Emunim, the Youth Faction became its unofficial spokesman within the party and the government.

Factional Relations and Coalitional Politics

As a camp-party the NRP is under particular pressure to enter into coalition governments with the dominant party. It represents a minority group characterized by distinctive values and behavioral patterns, interrelated through an extensive network of institutions. In order to protect its constituents and their interests, the NRP seeks to participate in the government. But other factors also operate that both encourage and restrain the NRP from such participation. A case study of the negotiations surrounding the formation of a government after the 1973 elections is instructive in this regard.

The Labor Party (formerly Mapai) dominated Israeli politics from the establishment of the state until the 1977 Knesset elections. In the mid-1960s it formed an electoral and parliamentary bloc with the small left-wing party Mapam and took the name "The Alignment." Hence, negotiations over formation of a government took place between the NRP and the Alignment following the 1973 elections.

The NRP presented three major demands: that the Law of Return be amended to stipulate that only those converted to Judaism in accordance with Orthodox law (i.e., not those converted in accordance with Conservative or Reform procedures) were to be recognized as Jews; that the government make no decision to withdraw from the occupied territories; and that the right-wing nationalist party, the Likud, be included in the coalition. It was understood that while the NRP would not insist that all three demands be satisfied, the Alignment would have to make substantial concessions. As we shall see, although the Alignment refused to comply with any of the demands, the NRP joined the coalition. But when Prime Minister Golda Meir resigned and was replaced by Yitzhak Rabin, the NRP refused to join his government. It reversed this decision a few months later and accepted the conditions it had previously rejected. It is these developments we wish to understand.

Let us begin by examining the NRP's three basic demands. The demand to amend the Law of Return had a history that began in January 1970, when the Supreme Court ruled that, for purposes of registration, a person's declaration that he was Jewish was sufficient evidence that he was a Jew. In the controversy that followed, the NRP obtained the Meir government's agreement to overrule the Court's decision by amending the Law of Return. The amendment defined a Jew as someone born of a Jewish mother or a convert to Judaism. But the law did not explicitly state that conversions had to be conducted in accordance with *halakha,* and heavy pressure was exerted on the NRP by influential rabbinical circles in Israel and the Diaspora to amend the law. Orthodox circles in the United States, for example, feared that the law strengthened the Conservative and Reform movements, since, at least by indirection, it recognized their conversions as valid.

The NRP recognizes the Chief Rabbinical Council as the supreme authority on matters of religion and *halakha*. Rabbi Isser Unterman, Ashkenazic chief rabbi in 1970, had fought for inclusion of the term "conversion in accordance with the *halakha*" in the original amendment. Despite his failure, both he and the Sephardic chief rabbi, Yitzhak Nissim, had authorized the NRP to remain in the government "under the existing circumstances." However, in 1973 the NRP convention declared that amending the Law of Return was a condition for participation in the government to be formed following the elections. The resolution admitted to more than one interpretation, but even the most permissive of them obliged party leaders to demonstrate some significant achievement before the party could enter a new coalition.

The other two demands were less influenced by outside pressures but were related to interfactional differences. At the 1973 party convention the Youth Faction and other hawks demanded that NRP participation in a coalition be contingent upon the new government's declaring that it would not withdraw from the West Bank. Party moderates, clearly in the minority, sought a nonoperative declaration proclaiming "our rights to all the land of Israel." The compromise statement declared that "the party refuses to take responsibility for a governmental peace agreement which concedes parts of the Homeland...."

NRP and Alignment negotiators agreed that new elections would be held before any final decision was made to withdraw from the West Bank. This formula left the hawks unhappy since the new government was now authorized to negotiate, though not execute, a withdrawal. New elections, they suspected, would only seal such an agreement. Their dissatisfaction may help account for the opposition of the Youth Faction to NRP participation in any government that did not include the Likud. Only such a government, they felt, would be sufficiently firm in negotiations with the Arabs. Both before and after the elections, the Youth Faction emphasized the importance of this point. However, NRP representatives in the coalition negotiations made it clear that the demand to include the Likud was not a condition for their joining the government. The negotiators had wide latitude in this respect. Although the NRP had campaigned on the platform of including the Likud in the new government, no party organ had ever made a binding decision in this regard.

The Youth Faction found itself allied with the new group Emunim, whose supporters also came primarily, though not exclusively, from the younger generation. Emunim, as we observed, was a transfactional alliance established before the 1973 elections. It was led by students and graduates of the Merkaz Harav Yeshiva and by religious settlers on the West Bank. Their spiritual guide was Rav Zvi Yehuda Kook. The real difference between Emunim and the Youth Faction was the former's single-minded concern with policy concerning the West Bank. In the 1973 elections many Emunim sympathizers actually voted for the Likud. (Emunim as we noted, eventually organized itself as a nonparty group called Gush Emunim, but many of its supporters retained membership in and personal ties to the NRP.)

It appears that having lost the fight within the NRP for a hawkish policy stance, the Youth Faction decided to sabotage NRP efforts to join the new coalition. With roughly 20 percent of the party vote, the Youth Faction could not expect the appointment of one of their members to the government. Whereas NRP membership in the government would strengthen the party in general, it was particularly desirable to those factions whose leaders would be appointed cabinet ministers. Control of a ministry meant prestige, funds, and patronage. Hence, if the NRP did not join the government, the Youth Faction's rivals would be weakened.

The Anatomy of a Religious Party

In order to achieve their goal the Youth Faction and Emunim concentrated their efforts on the "Who is a Jew?" issue. Spiritual leaders in both Israel and the Diaspora were far more anxious over the amendment of the Law of Return than they were over foreign policy issues. The Youth Faction insisted that unless the Alignment comply with NRP demands to amend the Law of Return (which they did not believe the Alignment would do), the NRP should refuse to enter a government that did not include the Likud. The rationale behind this demand was that the establishment of a government that included the Likud pointed to the existence of a national emergency that would justify overlooking the "Who is a Jew?" question.

The Youth and Emunim factions were supported in their demand by influential rabbinical figures in Israel and abroad. The result was to tie the hands of the NRP negotiators on an issue that, there is reason to believe, was a matter of relative indifference to leaders in the Youth Faction.

When it became evident, for reasons that need not concern us, that the Alignment would not concede on the "Who is a Jew?" issue, negotiators on both sides began to search for a compromise formula that would allow the NRP to point to some substantial achievement. After rejecting two proposals, NRP representatives finally agreed to a formula in which the coalition agreement would specify that "conversion is a *halakhic* term." A majority of the party's Central Committee, against the wishes of the Youth and Emunim groups, accepted the formula, conditional upon the agreement of the Chief Rabbinical Council. To everyone's surprise, that body refused to give its consent.

In fact, the moderates who thought they could coopt the chief rabbinate into their compromise and thereby add to its legitimacy had misjudged the position of the new Ashkenazic chief rabbi, Shlomo Goren. In the past Goren had extricated the NRP from a number of embarrassing political situations. One example was his lightning conversion of Helen Zeidman, who had already undergone a Reform conversion. Refusal to recognize her conversion had threatened to precipitate a government crisis until Goren resolved the issue. Party leaders mistakenly assumed that Goren, and the Chief Rabbinical Council in his wake, would come to their aid in the present difficulty, although they were under no obligation to consult them. Once the council issued a negative decision, NRP leaders felt obliged to follow its ruling. As a result, Prime Minister Golda Meir announced her intention of forming a minority government without the NRP.

Reports of the deteriorating situation on the Syrian border a few months later occasioned a new effort at compromise. NRP leaders declared that the emergency situation necessitated the immediate formation of a more stable government. The prime minister agreed to a declaration on behalf of the minister of the interior that since the amendment of the Law of Return in 1970, "no non-Jew had been registered as a Jew, and the government intended to continue in like fashion." NRP leaders represented this as an endorsement of Orthodox conversion, though no real basis for such an interpretation could be found in the declaration.

The NRP overcame both internal and external constraints and joined the government without having achieved its major demand. The Alignment compensated it with payoffs in other areas, for example, by increasing the number of its ministers from three to four, despite the party's loss of two mandates in the elections, and granting concessions in the area of religious education.

The agreement, however, was odious to many besides the Youth Faction. It appeared as a blatant surrender of religious principle in return for jobs. The Youth Faction representatives in the Knesset abstained from the vote of confidence for the new government. One veteran party leader refused to accept an appointment as minister and a second resigned from his post shortly after accepting appointment.

When Golda Meir resigned as prime minister (her resignation had no connection with the present issue), negotiations were automatically reopened for formation of a new government to be headed by Yitzhak Rabin. The NRP now decided not to join the coalition unless it received the blessings of the Chief Rabbinical Council. When no formula that satisfied both the Alignment and the Chief Rabbinical Council could be found, the NRP found itself in the opposition.

Five months later the NRP joined the Rabin government, accepting the same terms it had earlier rejected. The patterns of consociational politics were too strong. The NRP, representing a minority subculture, had institutional interests that it feared would be threatened if they remained outside the coalition for an extended period of time. Besides the economic benefits to be derived from participation in the government, they feared a repetition of the 1958-59 experience. At that time the NRP had also been in the opposition, and Mapai (the Labor Party's predecessor) had attempted to reduce NRP dominance in the Ministry of Religious Affairs and other quasi-governmental religious institutions. Threats in this direction were now sounded: there were even hints that the religious status quo was threatened. Finally, some NRP members (especially within the Youth Faction) who had originally opposed joining the coalition changed their position in order to give their party a policy-making voice in security and foreign affairs. Since the Likud was not to be included in the new government, they felt it was important to strengthen the hawkish wing of the Alignment by joining the coalition.

An additional point of interest worth noting is that religious issues as such were never the real center of the negotiations between the Alignment and the NRP, however things might have appeared on the surface. This was also true following the 1977 elections, when the Likud needed the NRP to form a government. The NRP received the long-coveted Ministry of Education and Culture and increased funding for its institutions in return for its support. But enhanced NRP influence in the new government did not result in substantial changes in the religious status quo. In the last analysis, the religious status quo is based not on arithmetical considerations but on the necessity of both religious and nonreligious sectors to settle their differences in a manner that both sides find tolerable. The Likud also needed Agudat Israel's support, but it was far less concerned than the NRP with the general shape of Israeli society or with its own image among the nonreligious public. Hence it felt greater freedom to press its arithmetic advantage, particularly after the 1981 elections. Agudat Israel's demands were so excessive that even the NRP took exception to them. However, precisely because Agudat Israel's primary concern was its own interests, its demands challenged but did not quite overturn the basic nature of the religious-nonreligious accommodation. On the other hand, Agudat Israel's achievements since 1977, from a religious point of view, have enhanced its reputation in the eyes of some religious voters who traditionally supported the NRP.

RELIGION AND POLITICAL ACTIVISM

The awakening of ultranationalist sentiments among religious Zionists followed the Six-Day and Yom Kippur wars. These wars quickened messianic expectations among religious Zionists and strengthened commitments to notions of a greater Israel. The impact of the two wars stemmed in part from the military victories, the liberation of Jerusalem and other "holy" cities, and the exercise of Israeli sovereignty over the entire West Bank. All this aroused great enthusiasm in religious circles, which attributed the outcome to the hand of God and saw it as a sign of imminent Redemption.

The Six-Day War had an impact on religious circles for other reasons as well. In the waiting period before the war, Israelis feared the outcome. This anxiety sharpened their senses of Jewish solidarity and of alienation and estrangement from the Gentile nations, who seemed unprepared to help them. The feeling that the nations of the world were prepared to surrender Israelis to their fate, as they had surrendered the Jews to the Holocaust, was reinforced by perceptions of the Yom Kippur War. The experience gave credence to the conceptions of spiritual leaders such as Rav Zvi Yehuda Kook, who warned Israelis that they must put their trust in God alone and act in accordance with His wishes rather than consider the advice and opinion of other nations.

The two wars strengthened the attraction of Rav Kook's expansionist philosophy in religious Zionist circles. More than ever, sacred value was attributed to national (Jewish) unity, which enhanced religious Zionist willingness to cooperate with nonreligious Jews. In addition, they sought to extend their involvement into broader social and political areas. The wars were not the only factors that led to this outcome. As we indicated, this sentiment was present among the Youth Faction, in particular, before the 1967 war. Religious Zionists had always accepted, in principle, the value of cooperation with nonreligious groups and their responsibility to engage in general social and political areas. But the readiness to do so, in practice, was restrained by pragmatic considerations. The NRP and the settlements associated with the NRP, for example, had never welcomed nonreligious members, and NRP political demands were generally limited to the protection of narrow religious interests.

The self-imposed isolation of religious Zionists, despite their ideology, was a result of a number of factors. It reflected their marginal position in Israeli society and culture. Religious Zionists represented a small minority of the population; initiative and leadership of the nation were in the hands of secularists. Labor Party leaders, in particular, set the tone in the country. Religious Zionists played the role of satellites, and this status led them to a policy of defensiveness and separatism in order to defend their own particular values and principles, lest they be overwhelmed by secular Zionism. Finally, as we noted, the older generation was somewhat estranged, by background and culture, from the secular society.

Following the two wars, members of the younger generation of religious Zionists, now in positions of influence, were prepared to engage secular Zionism in ideological confrontation and to extend their activity to all areas of society. Their weapons included the expansionist philosophy of Rav Kook, which reinterpreted Zionist ideology in the terminology of traditional Judaism, and their newly acquired status as standard-bearers of Jewish settlement on the West Bank and exemplars of Zionism's pioneering spirit. To their surprise, they found the battlefield empty.

During the prestate period and the early years of statehood, secularist leaders were often hostile toward or contemptuous of religious circles and the religious tradition. Secular energies were invested in the creation of a new Judaism or a reinterpretation of the tradition from a secular perspective. The best example of this approach is Labor Zionism, whose Zionist-socialist ideology formed the foundation of Israeli culture.

After the establishment of Israel, the ideology of secular Zionism, Zionist-Socialism in particular, declined in importance, and, as we noted in chapter four, the symbols of traditional Judaism increasingly penetrated the culture. These developments received added impetus after 1967 and increased the readiness of religious Zionist circles to absorb an ideology that sacralized the state and its institutions. These institutions, it was now believed, were no longer hostile to religion but open to its influence.

Following the Six-Day War, religious Zionists found that they were the segment in Israeli society that offered the most consistent support for a policy of retaining Israeli sovereignty over the occupied territories. Furthermore, they had an ideology that legitimated that policy. Among the secular Zionists, they found hesitation, weakness, and ideological confusion. For the first time since the beginning of modern Zionism, religious Zionists became the central force in settlement of the land, dictating policy through their political influence at the governmental level and through their quasi-legal settlement activity, which the government often legitimated after the fact.

These activities were projected from a religious perspective. Advocates stressed their special contribution as religious Jews. In addition, religious ultranationalism enabled religious Zionists to overcome their continuing sense of inferiority vis-à-vis Agudat Israel. The latter had traditionally charged the NRP with compromising religious principle and had posed as that principle's true defenders. Many religious Zionists accepted these charges as true. Now, however, religious Zionist ultranationalism was wrapped in the mantle of religious commandment, and its advocates, rather than Agudat Israel, could pose as the militant defenders of religious principle.

Within the religious Zionist camp, the younger generation had the greatest affinity with these currents. They had studied in religious high schools, where, beginning in the late 1950s, the expansionist ideology of Rav Zvi Yehuda Kook had increasingly prevailed. It was the Israeli-born generation whose perceptive apparatus had been conditioned to apprehend events initiated by the Six-Day War as confirmation of imminent Redemption. Furthermore, the younger generation was far less constrained by experience, personal ties, or caution in maintaining political alliances with the Labor Party and the policies of the past.

Since 1977 there has been some decline in the messianic activist orientation within religious Zionist circles and a return to a more pragmatic attitude in foreign affairs. This disposition was especially noticeable during the 1982 war in Lebanon. It is partly linked to events initiated by Sadat's visit to Jerusalem and the Camp David agreement and partly to the appointment of Youth Faction leaders to key posts in both the party and the government. The responsibility has had a restraining effect. Furthermore, the desire to maintain party unity (there are dovish elements in opposing factions) has had a moderating influence. Electoral considerations have also played a role. Youth Faction leaders are increasingly convinced that they cannot compete with either the Likud (the ruling coalition partner) or the new ultranationalist party, Hateḥiya, which has strong religious representation, for the allegiance of the religious voter whose overwhelming concern is support for a greater Israel. Hence, there is a tendency, from the standpoint of both factional and party considerations, to pay greater attention to the moderate religious voter, who is uneasy with the Youth Faction's militance. But as long as a substantial number of Gush Emunim sympathizers and West Bank settlers support the Youth Faction, the moderation of foreign policy positions within the NRP in general and the Youth Faction in particular will be limited. The ultranationalist settlers and youth movement members who share their orientations are accorded a deference that exceeds their electoral weight. They represent institutions and enterprises that are considered symbols of the religious Zionist movement, and as long as the NRP leadership is unwilling to surrender their support, or as long as they continue to identify with the NRP (as we shall see, some break in their attachment to the NRP has already occurred), the party will be pulled in a hawkish direction.

Recent Changes in the NRP's Electoral Support

In the 1977 elections the NRP increased its Knesset representation from ten to twelve seats. The new mandates came from a group best defined as "protest voters." The protest voters, at least until 1981, were part of the Youth Faction's constituency. In 1973 they expressed their dissatisfaction with the NRP leadership by voting for the Likud or for the extremist party headed by Rabbi Kahana,[4] whose goals included the expulsion of all Arabs from Israel. The Youth Faction's rise to a dominant position between 1973 and 1977 and NRP's adoption of a more militant nationalist platform encouraged these voters to return to the party.

There is a difference between the protest voters and other religiously observant Jews who vote for nonreligious parties. The latter, according to studies of voting behavior in Israel,[5] tend to be older Sephardic Jews who are members of trade unions and have low socioeconomic status. Their indifference to the religious parties is best explained by the fact that upon their arrival in Israel they were integrated into the organizational framework of the Labor movement. They are nonideological voters who constitute a social class quite different from the protest voters. The Sephardic religious voter who did not support the NRP tended to vote for the Labor Party until the 1970s.[6] In 1977 some of these voters, the younger elements in particular, switched to the Likud because they preferred its foreign policy and admired Begin. Many of the traditional NRP voters who moved to Tami in 1981 (to be discussed below) were part of the same social network and had the same social characteristics as those Sephardic voters who stayed outside the NRP framework.

The protest voters, young Israeli-born Ashkenazic Jews who tend to vote out of ideological conviction, supported right-wing political parties as early as 1973 and returned to the NRP in 1977 following its move to the right. They abandoned it again in 1981 in favor of the new ultranationalist party, Hateḥiya, or the Likud. The NRP, in fact, lost six mandates in the 1981 elections but only two from the protest voters. One went to Hateḥiya and one to the Likud. The loss to Hatehiya is explained by disappointment among the young ultranationalist elements with both the NRP and the Likud. This element opposed the Camp David agreement and vigorously objected to Israeli withdrawal from Sinai. They charged the Likud, and the NRP by indirection, with not devoting sufficient resources to assisting Jewish settlements on the West Bank.

There is, however, an important difference between the protest voters' support for the Likud in 1973 and for Hateḥiya in 1981. In the former case the protest voters constituted a marginal group of additional Likud voters. In the latter case they had become an important constituency of a new party that won only three seats in the election and that viewed itself as the voice of the Jewish settlements on the West Bank. Moreover, the ideology of the protest voters has been refined over the past decade. Basing themselves on interpretations of Rav Kook (both father and son) the protest voters posit that their political values, both their ultranationalism and their cooperation with secular nationalists in the Hateḥiya framework, are religious values no less important than the religious values and interests to which the NRP was traditionally dedicated. Hence, their move away from the NRP in 1981 is more firmly grounded in ideological terms than was their 1973 vote for the Likud. Furthermore, the support of the Likud (Prime Minister Begin, in particular) for broad religious interests and religious symbols has defused the traditional tensions and fears that religious voters harbored with regard to the government. Hence, it became relatively easy for religious voters to abandon the NRP, secure in the sense that the party was no longer needed to protect such interests as religious education or the religious status quo. A change in government policy in this regard could bring the protest voter back to the NRP.

It is ironic that the NRP suffered the most serious contraction of its voting constituency precisely in the period when Youth Faction leaders, now in commanding positions within the party, spoke of extending the ranks of NRP supporters beyond religious circles. They suggested the organization of a division of nonreligious supporters to enlist Israelis sympathetic to their general policies and favorable to traditional religious values. The NRP always attracted an estimated ten to fifteen thousand Arab voters. This fact is best explained by the favors and services that the party and its representatives in the government performed for selected Arabs. But the emergence of the Youth Faction and the development of policy programs in areas beyond those narrowly defined as religious seemed to open the way to attract nonreligious Jewish voters. Some analysts have drawn an analogy between the NRP and Christian Democratic parties. However, in 1981 the NRP lost many of its traditional supporters in the religious camp and won very few votes from the nonreligious.

We have already accounted for the defection of protest voters, which cost the NRP an estimated two Knesset seats. The loss of an additional four seats is explained by the defection of Sephardic voters, most of whom supported Tami, a new ethnic ticket headed by the NRP's former minister of religion, Aharon Abuḥatzera. Tami won three Knesset seats. Most of the remaining Sephardim who left the party supported the Likud.

In one respect Tami can be considered as simply another addition to the parties of the religious camp. Whereas Agudat Israel represents non-Zionist religious voters, Tami represents Sephardic voters in the religious camp. There is some truth to this assertion, but it is hardly the whole story. Tami played on the theme of ethnic discrimination, a concern that pervaded Israeli society in 1981 and affected voting for other parties as well. The arousal of ethnic sentiments was the necessary, but not the sufficient, condition for Tami's success. Because what is left unexplained is why Tami did not remain within the NRP as an organized faction.

There is a basic difference between the orientations of Sephardic and Ashkenazic voters toward the religious camp in general and the NRP in particular. This makes Tami something other than simply the religious camp-party of Sephardic Jews. In fact, Tami called itself a party of "traditionalist" rather than "religious" voters. On the whole, the religious Sephardi is less rigid and punctilious in observance, less doctrinaire in his religious beliefs, and less ideological in his religio-political values than the religious Ashkenazi. Sephardic voters in general, religious Sephardim in particular, are hawkish in foreign policy, but this stance is not the result of any religious ideology. Whether they are simply proud nationalists or xenophobes, their preferences are not grounded in religious conceptions about the sanctity of the land or messianic expectations. Hence, recent ideological changes within the NRP hardly aroused their sympathy, but the emphasis on ideology did suggest to them that primordial loyalties to fellow religionists were no longer governing considerations in NRP policy. On the other hand, as we indicated with respect to the protest voters, the Likud since 1977 has provided religious Jews, and certainly traditionalist Sephardic Jews, with a sense that their basic religious interests are no longer threatened.

The nature of the NRP's Sephardic constituents made it exceedingly difficult for them to organize as a separate faction within the party. The group, almost by definition, had no ideological program around which it could focus. Nonideology or less religious punctiliousness is hardly a banner with which to rally support. Ethnicity per se has never been a legitimate basis for political organization in Israel in general, and among the religious parties in particular. Common religious interests and shared values are supposed to make ethnic differences politically irrelevant. Ethnic appeals can and have struck spontaneous chords among Sephardic Jews in Israel and have provided the bases for large and sometimes violent demonstrations, but not for any enduring efforts. Finally, as we noted, all NRP factions have been sensitive to their ethnic composition in the last few years. Their response, for the most part, was to recruit a few Sephardim and coopt them in token positions. The masses of Sephardim retained a sense of continued frustration at numerical underrepresentation and absence of real influence, but the potential leaders of an ethnic faction were skimmed off. When the one leader with real authority, Aharon

Abuḥatzera, raised the banner of secession (and his own personal interests help account for his behavior), he found that many Sephardim, Moroccans in particular, flocked to him. (Abuḥatzera is a Moroccan, scion of one of its most famous rabbinical lines.)

Whether or not Tami voters return to the NRP depends not only on the rise or fall of ethnic consciousness in the next few years but on the development of the religious identity of the Sephardic voter. If this identity is sharpened, then they are likely to return to the NRP. If not, and if there is a relative absence of religious-secular tension, Tami's voters may not only remain outside the NRP, but many of them may gradually dissociate from the religious camp as well.

What remains to be emphasized is that the legitimation of the defection of both protest voters and Sephardic voters is an unintended consequence of the Youth Faction's activity. The Youth Faction stressed the importance of ideology and emphasized the desirability of religious Zionist involvement in broader social issues. It is doubtful if Youth Faction leaders appreciated the implications of what they were demanding. The stress on ideology meant relegating the economic, social, and even familial ties that bound the religious Zionist to his camp-party to a secondary position. Emphasizing engagement in broad social, economic, and political issues, rather than the defense of narrow religious interests, suggested that defense of the camp was not a primary concern. This attitude further undermined loyalty and solidarity within the camp and encouraged those unhappy with the specific direction of NRP policy to vote for other parties.

– 8 –

Religious Extremism in Israel

Orthodox Jewish ideologies, as our previous chapters suggest, can be broadly subdivided into those which reject modernity, whose followers we call neo-traditionalists, and those which affirm modernity, whose followers we call modern Orthodox.[1]

NEO-TRADITIONALISM

The Orthodox rejection of modernity is a strategy, a by-product of the effort to retain the observance of Jewish law and its integrity. Whereas religion in traditional societies is in harmony with the surrounding culture and is buttressed by, as it in turn buttresses, the social reality and perceptions of the society in which it is rooted, neo-traditionalism must reconstitute the perception of its adherents in opposition to the surrounding culture. This process, however, also impinges on traditionalist perceptions and expectations. Most striking is the fact that neo-traditional religious societies are less religiously permissive and far less tolerant of breaches in religious observance than are traditional societies.

What specific aspects of modernity do the neo-traditionalists reject? There were and are differences among them in the extent to which they seek to insulate themselves from modernity. For example, not all of them oppose all forms of secular education. What is true of all of them is that even if they legitimate secular education, they do so in instrumental, primarily economic terms.

There are also differences of opinion among neo-traditionalists about the proper attitude to be adopted toward nonreligious Jews. The contro-

This chapter is based on an article in Hebrew by Charles S. Liebman, "The Rise of Neo-Traditionalism among Orthodox Jews in Israel," *Megamot* 27 (May 1982): 231–50.

versy is limited on the one hand by religious injunctions that assert that a Jew, even though he sins, remains a Jew and that all Jews are responsible for one another's behavior. On the other hand, association with nonreligious Jews poses various problems, including the violation of a host of injunctions against association with evil-doers. Neo-traditionalist groups and leaders have adopted various strategies for dealing with nonreligious Jews, but they are all characterized by the sense that a vast spiritual and behavioral gap separates the Orthodox from the non-Orthodox.

Neo-traditionalists counterpose their own world view, which they are convinced is the only authentic one, with those aspects of the modern world which they reject, arranging the oppositions along four axes: authority-anarchy, absolutism-relativism, bodily control–bodily license, purposefulness-meaninglessness. The neo-traditionalist tendency, other things being equal, is to broaden continually the scope of *halakha*. *Halakha* is interpreted by rabbinic masters (experts in Talmudic study), whose authority is absolute. Logic and rationality are highly esteemed but only within the context of the authority of the legal code and traditional rabbinical interpretation. The neo-traditionalist aspires to a life directed toward holiness and purity. By definition, observance of God's law and study of His revealed scripture brings one closer to God, the source of holiness and purity. This observance requires great self-control. Temptations, especially in the realm of sexual behavior, always exist. Under modern conditions, the temptations reflected in the mass communications media, in the manner in which women dress and conduct themselves, in the social and physical contact between the sexes that modern Western society takes for granted, lead to impure thought if not impure action. Strict separation of the sexes and avoidance of the mass media are helpful in the constant struggle to overcome these temptations. Since the modern world is characterized by ever greater sexual license, ordinances governing separation and avoidance must be ever more rigidly adhered to. (There are additional reasons for avoiding contact with secular culture in general and the mass media in particular. They challenge religious tenets at a variety of levels. At best they waste time that could be devoted to the study of sacred texts.) The virtuous life is one lived in accordance with Jewish law and devoted, as far as possible, to the study of sacred texts. It is the ultimate life of meaning and is not only a religious obligation but becomes, in time, the fulfillment of one's self and the realization of one's purpose. Hence, the Orthodox Jew is truly blessed and rewarded. Whatever else he may think of the non-Orthodox Jew, the neo-traditionalist also pities him.

Modernity has led the more extreme and consistent of the neo-traditionalists to create structures and institutions to prevent its penetration. This undertaking often requires the duplication or imitation of technically advanced instrumentalities so that they can be shorn of their overt antireligious effects. (For example, there are buses for transporting neo-traditionalists to work in which seating is segregated by sex, and sexually offensive advertisements are eliminated.) The effort to exploit modern technology and/or politics for the religious needs of neo-traditionalists may seem naïve to contemporary social scientists, who argue that political mobilization and technological advances bear the seeds of modern consciousness. Nevertheless, Jewish neo-traditionalism, as we shall see, has shown a remarkable vitality. Its point of view in Israel is associated with a variety of groups, ranging from the numerically small Neturei Karta (Guardians of the Wall), whose members vigorously oppose the existence of a secular Jewish state, to Agudat Israel, which receives support from about 5 percent of Israeli voters (though not all its supporters are neo-traditionalists).

Modern Orthodoxy: The Affirmation of Modernity

There are three ideal-typical responses of modern Orthodoxy to the challenges that modernity poses to Jewish observance and rabbinic authority. Each of these responses seeks to preserve *halakha* while avoiding social and cultural insulation from the modern world.

One response, adaptationism, affirms that the basic values of modernity not only are compatible with Judaism but partake of its essence. Freedom, equality of man, rationalism, science, rule of law, etc. are all found to be inherent in the Jewish tradition. Secular study is affirmed as a positive religious value—an instrument whereby man might learn more of God's creation. Not least important, adaptationism includes an effort to reinterpret the tradition, including those aspects of the law which seem to stand in opposition to modern values.

A second response, compartmentalization, seeks to preserve the tradition untouched, but defines some aspects of life that it regards as religiously or Jewishly neutral as legitimately subject to the influence of modernity. From one perspective, compartmentalization involves a radical transformation in traditional assumptions about what is or is not religiously relevant. From another perspective, compartmentalization is a reactionary response; it seeks to seal some aspects of life from the influence of the modern world.

The third response, expansionism, affirms modernity by reinterpreting it through the prism of the Jewish tradition.[2] It aspires, in theory, to bring all aspects of life under the rubric of its interpretation of Judaism. The most significant contemporary version of expansionism is expressed by the disciples of Rav Zvi Yehuda Kook in Gush Emunim and their sympathizers, whose principles include commitment to Jewish nationalism, a redefinition of secular Zionism to render it compatible with their effort to incorporate all Jewish nationalists within their framework, and the belief that divine Redemption is imminent.

The Decline of Modern Orthodoxy in Israel

The most dramatic development in religious life in Israel during the last decade has been the apparent retreat of modern Orthodoxy and the strengthening of neo-traditionalist tendencies. This growth has been observed among non-Israeli Jews,[3] but it is more striking in Israel, given the history of tension between neo-traditionalism and Zionism.

Many modern Orthodox Israelis are disturbed by the increase in what they call "religious extremism," particularly among the younger generation. They are especially troubled by it when their own children are involved. Religious extremism has two reflections: one in neo-traditionalism, as we have defined it, and the second in the reformulation of the expansionist response in a nationalistically radical, but otherwise neo-traditional, outlook. Five aspects of religious extremism are particularly disturbing to the older modern Orthodox Israelis.

First is the increased rigor of religious observance. Strict observance of *halakha* among modern Orthodox Israelis in general appears to be increasing. For example, many married women who never before observed the injunction to cover their hair in public now do so even in their own homes. But the degree of increased observance by some, particularly younger, Orthodox Jews and the symbolic import of what they tend to emphasize connote a whole different level of observance. Dietary laws are a good example. These laws have always been of great importance, for they carry implications about whom one can effectively sit with at a dinner table. Jewish schismatics are readily identified by their assertion of new dietary restrictions. Now there are differences, seemingly minor ones, between neo-traditionalists and modern Orthodox Jews with respect to dietary regulations. But these differences are of enormous symbolic import, for they generally revolve around the issue of whether one accepts modern Orthodox or neo-traditionalist rabbinical authority. One difference in particular, which has to do with whether one can partake of fruits grown during a certain period, has divided religious Zionists from neo-traditionalists during this century. Thus, the fact that increasing numbers of ostensibly modern Orthodox Jews have adopted the neo-traditionalists' prohibition is very disturbing to some.

In this same regard, there are Jewish laws that most modern Orthodox Jews recognize as binding but that many of them violate or ignore. The prohibition against men and women bathing together is one such example. (There are a few modern Orthodox rabbis—fewer today than in the past —who sanction "mixed swimming.") The pattern of increased observance of these laws, particularly on the part of young people raised in Orthodox homes where such laws are not observed, is threatening to the religious identity of the parents and seems to them to carry overtones of neo-traditionalism, even though today's expansionists are no less rigorous in their observance of such regulations. In many areas, most especially those which prohibit virtually all contact or association between unmarried men and women, expansionist leaders have accepted the prohibitions of the neo-traditionalists and have encouraged many young people to do so as well. As far as the modern Orthodox Jews who are troubled by this development are concerned, it makes no difference whether neo-traditionalist patterns are operating directly on young people, or whether neo-traditionalism is penetrating the ranks of modern Orthodoxy through changes in the ideology and world view of expansionist leaders. Many "extremist" patterns, as we shall see, are also associated with expansionism. In fact, neo-traditionalists in Israel refer to themselves and are referred to by others as *hareydim* (sing. *hareydi*), which is best translated as pious. In contrast, modern Orthodox Jews, as we know, refer to themselves as *datiim,* which means religious. Many now use the term *hareydi l'umi* (nationalistic-pietist) to refer to the expansionists. The term implies that the principal difference between the expansionists and the neo-traditionalists is in the formers' affirmation of Zionism. But, some maintain, there is a dynamic to religious extremism that leads from expansionism to neo-traditionalism. According to the leader of B'nei Akiva, the religious-Zionist youth movement:

> The new concept, nationalistic-pietist, will lead to developments that will be impossible to prevent; primarily the deepening of Torah education and a lessening of secular education. Wherever, in the Jewish world, there is Torah to the exclusion of everything else, the negative element—anti-Zionism—has also appeared. . . . This is religious extremism—separating young men and women, preventing secular education, and anti-Zionism.[4]

The second aspect of extremism that modern Orthodox Jews find disturbing relates to the declining role of familial custom. There have always been some variations in Jewish practices among different communities. The *halakha* itself recognizes the legitimacy of these variations and lays great stress on the sanctity of custom. Customs tend to be familial, though they can also be communal. One of the most troubling aspects to many modern Orthodox Jews in the rise of extremism is the uniformity that is demanded in the interpretation of *halakha*—a uniformity that overrides custom and, therefore, destroys local and familial traditions and breaks down parental religious authority. This aspect of extremism characterizes expansionists more than neo-traditionalists, though similar tendencies are evident in the latter community as well. The expansionists seek to impose uniform standards on their mostly young adherents and show almost studied indifference to older people in general and to familial traditions in particular—an attitude that is not entirely surprising, given the radical thrust of the expansionist message.

The third manner in which "extremism" disturbs many modern Orthodox Jews is in its monist point of view. Most modern Orthodox Jews in Israel, without regard to their religious ideology, relate to the world in a compartmentalized manner. In other words, whatever most of them think they ought to be doing in theory, they know and accept as entirely fitting that in practice they relate to some aspects of life (e.g., prayer, dietary or sabbath observance) as religious Jews and to others (e.g., secular culture, economic activity, politics) as modern men and women. Leaders of the National Religious Party, for example, traditionally distinguished between religio-political questions, such as the legal definition of who is a Jew or whether buses and theaters should operate on the Sabbath, and general political questions, such as foreign or economic policy. They assumed that the latter had nothing intrinsically to do with religion and that support in this realm could be bargained away for support in the religio-political realm. Today, increasing numbers of young people raised in modern Orthodox homes have rejected this multiple identity. For example, during the period of their opposition to the party leadership in the 1960s and early 1970s, the Youth Faction of the National Religious Party maintained that all political questions ought to be resolved from a religious perspective. The Youth Faction was influenced by an expansionist point of view, and some see the spread of religious monism as an indication of the increased strength of a rigorous expansionist position. Others feel it presages a turn to neo-traditionalism. The latter point of view finds support in changing attitudes on the part of many young

Orthodox Jews toward secular education. While expansionists, as we will observe, show no great reverence toward secular education, they are not hostile to it as are Israeli neo-traditionalists. The latter reject any study except that devoted to sacred text. This attitude seems to characterize a growing number of young people. In other words, rejection of secular study implies a neo-traditional rather than an expansionist monism.

A fourth, related aspect of extremism that all modern Orthodox Jews, expansionists in particular, find disturbing is the degree to which some young people deny religious significance to the existence of the state of Israel. The decision, for example, to continue one's study at neo-traditional yeshivot rather than to serve in the army reflects a system of values that stresses study of sacred texts to the exclusion of other activities—even defending the state of Israel. The young people from modern Orthodox backgrounds who study in neo-traditional yeshivot whom we interviewed are not opposed to the existence of Israel. They feel, for the most part, that their religious study is of greater merit than army service—that they are an elite whom society ought to free from military duty so that they might prepare themselves to become Talmudic authorities. Many of them also feel that army service, either by its very nature or by the contact with secularists that it entails, is corrupting to a young person. Underlying the various arguments we heard for eliminating army service or shortening it by special exemption to a period of six months was the sense that however important Israel and its continued existence might be, those considerations were not ultimate Jewish values. A notion that was unexpressed in any of our interviews, though it is sometimes stated by neo-traditionalist apologists, was that by continuing their Talmudic studies rather than serving in the army, young men were insuring that God would protect Israel. Hence they were performing the greatest service to the state since, in the last analysis, it is God and not the army who assures the state's defense.

The final aspect of extremism that disturbs many modern Orthodox Jews is the style and orientation of religious observance and the world view that accompanies an extremist posture. There is a very apt expression that identifies young men or women overcome by religious enthusiasm. They become *nisrafim* (burned), a term that has its analogues in other religions, such as the "burned over districts" in the United States, which were swept by religious revivals in the nineteenth century. We find this expression especially meaningful because, although there is no Hebrew counterpart, the religious behavior and identity of most modern Orthodox is aptly described by the term "cool." That is, the characteristic modern Orthodox behavior pattern seems to be the detached manner in which one performs one's religious obligations. The knitted *kippa* (skullcap) declares one's identity as part of the religious camp. Everything one does demonstrates that the *kippa* really makes no difference. There is no display of religious observance; it is almost as though religion were being observed in secret—in secret even from oneself—as though the religious act were dissociated from one's personality. This "cool" style permits one to move with ease from one role (e.g., religious observance) to another (e.g., socializing). This pattern is evident, for example, in a synagogue, where one can hear the most mundane and profane of discussions periodically interrupted by the recitation of prayers. The incongruity of turning from a prayer that describes, for example, God in heaven surrounded by angels, to a discussion of politics, the stock market, sports, or sex does not seem to deter such behavior.

"Cool" is not an exclusively modern Orthodox style, nor the enthusiasm of the "burned" an exclusively neo-traditional one. One finds "cool" neo-traditional Jews. Their ostensible detachment is especially striking when they are in special garb and employ the distinctive gestures and mannerisms that identify them as "pious." On the other hand, the expansionists express the epitome of a "burned" style. Hence it is not style that distinguishes neo-traditionalists from modern-Orthodox. But the enthusiasm of the "burned" ones is such a radical departure from the norms of urbanity and modernity to which most modern-Orthodox have become accustomed, that they associate it with a neo-traditional posture, i.e., withdrawal from the world.

Factors Leading to the Growth of Religious Extremism

The growth of extremism among the modern Orthodox Jews can be explained, first of all, by the inability of the various modern Orthodox interpretations to compete with the world view of neo-traditionalism, or, in other words, the failure of modern Orthodoxy to demonstrate that modernity and Judaism are in fact compatible.

The adaptationist response, other things being equal, seems compromising and lacking in authenticity to many modern Orthodox Jews. We must remember that Orthodoxy defines proper Jewish life as adherence to Jewish law. Hence, the more precisely and rigidly one adheres to the law, the better Jew one becomes. While the adaptationists argue that their interpretation of Jewish law is no less valid than that of the neo-traditionalists and strict constructionists, their case is weak. First of all, no recognized Talmudic authorities are identified with their approach. Hence reformists must engage not only in a fight over the interpretation of the Judaic tradition, in which the logic of their position might or might not be persuasive, but in an argument over the nature of rabbinic authority, in which, as in any religion, the conservative side has a clear advantage. Second, it is difficult for the adaptationists to escape the charge that their "reforms" are motivated by their attraction to the modern secular world rather than by their commitment to what is Jewishly authentic. Third, the adaptationists are at a competitive disadvantage with the neo-traditionalists. The former recognize the legitimacy of the latter's interpretation of Jewish law but demand legitimacy for their interpretation as well. In other words, they pose a pluralist model of interpretation. The neo-traditionalists, on the other hand, deny the legitimacy of the reformists' conceptions, which provides them with a distinct psychological advantage.

Compartmentalization as an ideology never struck roots in Israel. It has been adopted by most Orthodox Jews as an unselfconscious strategy mediating between the demands of *halakha* and the desire to live as part of the modern world. Their behavior is characterized by de facto compartmentalization—multiple identities through which they relate to different aspects of life. One can find legitimation for this point of view in the Diaspora. The dominant cultural model there encourages the distinction between one's religious identity and one's orientation to economic, political, and even many social and cultural aspects of life. But it seems naïve to define culture, society, and political institutions as matters of Jewish irrelevance in Israel.

Expansionism seems to be the most suitable modern Orthodox response in Israel. It affirms *halakha* with rigor, it possesses an inclusive world view, and it is ostensibly compatible with both Jewish nationalism and modernity. Following the Six-Day War in June 1967, it appeared as though expansionist orientations would dominate all of Orthodoxy. Theoretically, at least, expansionism certainly prevailed among the modern Orthodox Israelis. It is associated with the ideology of Gush Emunim, which has established a number of settlements on the West Bank. Expansionist adherents appeared to be on the verge of controlling the National Religious Party in the early 1970s. Its philosophy, as least until recently, dominated both the religious Zionist youth movement and the yeshiva high school movement. In the last few years, those associated with the expansionist ideology have opened schools at both the elementary and college levels, in addition to two new high schools that are more rigorously associated with their social and political point of view. What has happened, however, is that as expansionism elaborated itself, it adopted more and more characteristics of neo-traditionalism.

Indeed, it may be fair to characterize expansionism today as a nationalist version of neo-traditionalism. For example, its leaders have rejected secular studies, humanistic ones in particular, in their school curricula.[5] They have retained certain basic values of modernity that distinguish them from the neo-traditionalists. They do not prohibit reading newspapers, watching television, or attending concerts, the theater, etc., although they do make efforts to channel leisure time into sacred study. In other words, they are far less prone than the neo-traditionalists to insulate themselves from cultural and social influences of modern society, despite growing signs of impatience with Western civilization. Their attitude toward the non-Jewish and non-Israeli world has become increasingly disdainful. The issue of proper dress has gained in importance, and appropriate relations between the sexes are a matter less and less of subjective feeling and more and more of codified halakhic standards of conduct. On the other hand, women are assigned important roles in political activity, they are encouraged to study sacred texts, and, as far as one can tell, they are treated as social equals. Finally, and most important, the expansionists continue to cooperate with nonobservant Jews who are willing to join with them in their nationalist efforts. While it is true that this cooperation is purely tactical for some, it is a matter of principle for others. These expansionists refuse to recognize the conception of secular nationalism, arguing that Jewish nationalists are by definition fulfilling the most important religious commandments and hence are more suitable partners than the antinationalist neo-traditionalists. This cooperation is, as we shall suggest, a serious problem for the growth of expansionism.

The growth of religious extremism, expressed in both neo-traditionalism and expansionism, is attributable to more than the failure of adaptationism or compartmentalization. The fact is that the basic thrust of religious extremism is compatible with the structure of Orthodox thought and institutions.[6] It reflects some of the consequences—intentional and unintentional—of their operation. The compatibility of extremism and Orthodoxy is best understood by a closer look at Orthodox educational institutions.

Lawrence Kaplan has suggested that modern Orthodox yeshiva high schools, in adopting the "narrow, particularistic, authoritarian emphases" of the neo-traditional yeshiva curriculum, have undermined their own ideology.[7] His suggestion can be pushed further. The very structure of the yeshiva, its isolation and segregation from the outside world in general and from nonreligious Jews in particular, and the strict division within the curriculum of secular and sacred subjects promotes extremist orientations regardless of the content of the curriculum. The prism through which the yeshiva world views reality reinforces a sense of sharp contrasts and distinctions. The category of holy, with its sharp distinction between pure and impure, like the categories of *halakha,* with their rigid boundaries between the permitted and the forbidden, reinforces a view of reality emphasizing separations and distinctions between objects or actions. The world is not a place where secular and profane, good and evil, Jew and non-Jew, religious and nonreligious interact, overlap, mesh, and blend. And if they do, they should not. The yeshiva is a place where reality, like behavior, is divided into good or evil, and distinctions are emphasized, not blurred. Indeed, yeshivot even distinguish between ostensibly observant and nominally religious Jews who are immersed in worldliness and secular pursuits, and religious Jews who strive to live in a world of holiness, purity, and sanctity. The classic distinction of the neo-traditional yeshiva world, which extends to high-school yeshivot as well, is not the distinction between Jew and non-Jew, or even between secular and religious Jew, but between the *ben-Torah* (literally the son of Torah), a category that refers less to scholarly achievement than to immersion in the world of learning, holiness, and purity, and the *baal-bayit* (literally the homeowner, i.e., the layman), who may be quite punctilious in his religious observance but whose orientation is toward secular matters. Such a world view makes the expansionist philosophy that blurs religious-nonreligious distinctions difficult to accept but does sustain its conceptions of a permanently hostile non-Jewish world in general and Arab world in particular. Indeed, religious Zionism, which affirms the positive contribution of nonreligious Jews, is suspect in all its formulations. Finally, religious Zionism requires an orientation toward the importance of involvement in *this* world, which contrasts with everything else the yeshiva world affirms about ultimate reality and ultimate values.

The paradox is that the high-school yeshivot were created because neo-traditional institutions were presumed inadequate and ideologically unacceptable by the religious Zionists. But the religious Zionists also favored "total" institutions to socialize the students to the values of modern Orthodoxy by isolating them from a worldly secular environment. Unlike many neo-traditional yeshivot where students may live at home, perhaps because they don't fear the home environment, most high-school yeshivot are dormitory schools. Students visit home once every three weeks, from Friday afternoon till Sunday morning. This isolation weans the student away from modern Orthodoxy, regardless of the school's curriculum or the orientations of the teacher. For in isolating itself, the yeshiva is making a statement about itself and its unique spirituality, about the study of sacred texts, and about the rest of society. The isolation and segregation of the yeshiva is by definition a statement about the supreme importance of sacred study and the life lived within the yeshiva walls in contrast to the life of the world. The continuation of this world view is found in the neo-traditional community, and that is where disproportionate numbers of the most committed and successful students are likely to be attracted. Others, who remain in the community of modern Orthodoxy, feel a sense of guilt and inadequacy and a desire to replicate as much as possible the patterns of neo-traditionalism.

Separation and distinction are characteristic of the halakhic legal system that lies at the heart of the Jewish world view. It stands to reason that boundaries and differences would characterize any system of order, and this feature seems to be especially true of the Judaic, certainly of the Mishnaic, world view.[8] (The Mishnah constitutes the basic document around which the Talmud is built.) It is a world view reinforced by other aspects of Israeli society, where religious and nonreligious Jews are increasingly separated and distinguished from one another. Modern Orthodox Jews are more segregated from nonreligious Jews today than in the past.[9] Neighborhoods in urban areas increasingly comprise large numbers of Orthodox Jews or none at all. Except in certain sections of Jerusalem or B'nei B'rak, there are few if any pure Orthodox neighborhoods. But individual multistory apartment houses or even clusters of such homes may be limited to religious Jews. There are enough Orthodox Jews on a street so that preschool-age children from religious homes can play almost exclusively with other religious children. Once the youngsters reach nursery or kindergarten age, segregation by type of school (religious or nonreligious) virtually assures homogeneous play groups. The same is true of adult friendship groups. There are few opportunities for religious and nonreligious couples to meet at a social level, and they are unlikely to feel comfortable in one another's presence. Much socializing among secular couples takes place on Friday night. Both nonreligious and religious Jews would be ill at ease when problems arose over observing the Sabbath (for example, whether or not to use electricity, to cook with a gas stove, or to smoke). Socializing among religious couples is more likely to take place on Saturday night within friendship groups formed through participation in the local synagogue or the local religious school, in groups that are continuations of those first formed in the B'nei Akiva youth movement, or even in semisocial study groups organized and sponsored by the National Religious Party.

Compulsory army service once brought religious and nonreligious youth together. Religious youth today increasingly serve in separate units in a variety of military frameworks that limit opportunity for intimate contact between religious and secular soldiers.[10]

Thus, even modern Orthodox Jews in Israel who feel they participate in contemporary society and are disdainful of the deliberate self-segregation of the neo-traditionalists find that many of their contacts with secularists and with contemporary culture are mediated by institutions composed exclusively of religious Jews. These institutions, regardless of their explicit ideology, shape a world view that rests on categories of segregation and distinction. The perception of the secular Jew as an "outsider," as essentially hostile, indeed as the equivalent of the *goy* (non-Jew; pl. *goyim*), if not the antisemite, is frequently expressed. *Ha'Aretz,* Israel's most prestigious newspaper, whose columns and editorials are often hostile to the political demands of the religious parties, is referred to in religious circles as an antisemitic paper. This is all part of an underlying perception of reality that promotes neo-traditional orientations but presents difficulties for expansionism.

The number of formerly modern Orthodox Jews in Israel who are now identified with neo-traditional institutions or practices may number no more than a few thousand, but they illustrate deeper trends reflected in the behavior of many modern Orthodox Jews and modern Orthodox institutions. While we have sought to explain this phenomenon in terms of the religious dynamic itself, it can only be understood by assuming that one is committed to *halakha* as an absolute value, and hence that one's commitment to the values and ideals of modernity is at best secondary and is contingent on their consistency with *halakha.* This value orientation itself merits examination.

There are two aspects of this perspective to be considered: the attraction of *halakha* and the problematics of modernity. Individuals and societies differ in the importance they ascribe to religious ritual. Ritual expresses our sense of order. According to Mary Douglas, ritual is most highly developed and symbolic action believed to be most efficacious in those cultures where man perceives himself as intimately related to society, as lacking autonomy and individual freedom—where the social group grips its members in tight communal bonds.[11] Personal autonomy, the breakdown of the individual's sense of group dependence, means a movement away from ritual and toward greater ethical concern. As we have already suggested, the Orthodox community has retained a remarkable vitality in Israel. Indeed, the great achievement of modern Orthodoxy and religious Zionism was the creation of an indigenous Orthodox community when it appeared to many in the 1930s and the 1940s that it might well disappear under the pressures of modernization and the attraction of secular Zionist ideologies. This Orthodox community in Israel is quite appropriately referred to as a "camp," with its own school system, political parties, youth groups, newspapers, economic institutions, and an intensive social-familial network mediating between religious Jews and the larger society. It is an overarching presence, and it is entirely consistent with Douglas to find that its members reify that society in a ritual system that appears natural and efficacious to them. There is an interrelationship in which the commitment to *halakha* requires a communal structure and the communal structure reinforces the commitment to *halakha*. This reinforcement is not primarily imposed externally or coercively. If it were, it might lead to efforts to mitigate its severity and rigor. On the contrary, it arises from within the individual. It is an expression of the individual's sense of community ties and responsibility and leads to ever stricter internal demands.

One might well ask why this process is so recent. (It is present in the neo-traditional community, which is having its set of difficulties with its own extremists.) One possible answer is that two important constraints that existed in the past no longer exist today. Rigorous interpretation and demands for strict observance of the law were mitigated by the responsibility that rabbinic leaders felt to include every Jew under their sway—the ignorant as well as the learned, the poor as well as the rich, the marginal as well as the well integrated. This is no longer the case. Precisely because Jews can and do opt out of the essentially voluntaristic Orthodox community, rabbinic leaders need answer only to the totally committed. But this was also true twenty and thirty years ago, when no evidence existed for the growth of religious extremism.

The second constraint that no longer exists is the economic one. Relative prosperity and political access to public funding has occasioned opportunities for extended yeshiva study, for greater leisure time, and for greater autonomy from the nonreligious institutional pressures that reinforced modern values and behavior. In addition, it has enabled religious leaders to interpret Jewish law in a more rigorous manner than was heretofore possible without causing serious hardship to the religiously committed Jewish community.

We are not certain why the Yom Kippur War was a turning point in the growth of neo-traditionalism in Israel, why trends already present in

Israel were vastly accelerated after 1973.[12] It is possible that neo-traditionalism had been on the rise since 1948, as the modern Orthodox community became more firmly established economically, politically, culturally, and, above all, educationally. In other words, once a religious community achieves a measure of autonomy, the religious dynamic itself leads to extremism. But in Israel, this dynamic was constrained by neo-traditionalist opposition to Zionism and their (at best) neutral attitude toward the state. Nationalism was so deeply ingrained within the modern Orthodox Jews that they had no tolerance for neo-traditionalism. But the decline of national morale, the sense of the disintegration of Israel as a moral community since the Yom Kippur War,[13] has opened the door to the political as well as the religious conceptions of neo-traditionalism. Now even its narrower religious conceptions are a significant reference point. Modern Orthodoxy was always troubled by the fact that its own position defied most of the rabbis associated with neo-traditionalism. One justification of such defiance was the argument that if these rabbinical authorities could be so wrong about Zionism, how could their judgment be trusted on other issues? After the Yom Kippur War, it was no longer so clear to all the modern Orthodox Jews that the neo-traditional judgment of Zionism had been wrong.

Expansionism also became an attractive option after the Six-Day War, particularly after the 1973 Yom Kippur War. It has benefited from the same causes that led to the rise of neo-traditionalism. There are also factors peculiar to Israel's international and domestic condition that account for the growth of expansionism and its primary political expression, Gush Emunim. We elaborated upon this topic in the previous chapter. But we must recall that religious extremism is incompatible with the expansionists' redefinition of secular Zionism and of nationalist secularist behavior. This is a troublesome point, well reflected in the reluctance of most religious ultranationalists to identify with the new political party Hateḥiya, although this party most accurately expresses the political and social ideology of Gush Emunim and the original West Bank settlers.

THE POLITICAL OPTIONS FOR RELIGIOUS EXTREMISTS

Religious groups, deeply committed to what they assume are ultimate truths and right behavior, face one of two choices: to attempt to impose their position on others or to withdraw as best they can from the world and attempt to preserve their own purity. The choice depends on a number of factors, including the cost of each strategy and its relative likelihood of success, the general political orientation of the religion out of which the group emerged and the group's own theological and social orientation, and the specific nature of the group's goals.

Religious extremist groups in Israel have chosen both options. The neo-traditional political orientation is primarily defensive. It seeks to withdraw rather than capture the world. Its major enemies are the secular Jews; the major threats to its integrity stem from Israeli society and culture. Hence its concern is to erect barriers. But precisely because its primary concern is preserving its own integrity by living a life of religious purity, its major thrust is really nonpolitical. Politics per se is devalued. It does not command most of the energies or attention of the neo-traditionalist elite since, by definition, politics is not what the good life, the religious life, is all about. One who devotes himself to politics cannot devote himself to the study of sacred texts and cannot, therefore, be numbered among the elite. Even such routine political participation as voting is not assigned significant religious value. Hence, one problem of Agudat Israel is that while it is the political arm of a religious camp, not all the camp followers bother to support it.[14]

Nevertheless, the neo-traditional world cannot avoid politics entirely. The state of Israel, like other modern states, is involved in providing health, education, and welfare services, in establishing, subsidizing, and funding various economic enterprises, in directing the economy through legislation and monetary policy, and in maintaining internal as well as external security. No group can effectively sever its links with society. The withdrawal itself, the erection of defensive barriers, requires political attentiveness by the leadership and mobilization of support to effectuate political demands. On the other hand, we must not forget that in the case of Agudat Israel this is a politics not of choice but of necessity. Those who choose to identify with the neo-traditional world are certainly not attracted by its political involvement. They have made a choice to withdraw from the modern-secular world, which includes eschewing of politics. Hence, it is well to bear in mind that while religion is involved in Israeli politics, it is, in the case of one extremist group, involved despite itself. Living the religious life to its fullest involves the curtailment if not the elimination of this involvement.

In contrast to neo-traditionalism, expansionism is political by definition. Obviously, it seeks the expansion of the spirit, but politics is more than a major instrument in its realization. Nationalism—not only the deepening of nationalist commitment but the achievement of nationalist goals, particularly settling and retaining the West Bank—has been raised to the level of a prime if not the prime religious objective. In addition, since the expansionists conceive of all human activity as capable of bearing sacred meaning, politics can certainly become a legitimate vocation. Rav Zvi Yehuda Kook himself encouraged his disciples on occasion to forego their studies in order to participate in political efforts. Finally, politics is integrated into religion by imposing religious symbols on its processes. Strictly speaking, Zvi Yehuda Kook did not urge his students to engage in politics but to carry out religious commandments such as settling the land or even attending political demonstrations. When Israel returned the oil fields of Abu-Rhodes to Egypt in the early stages of the fulfillment of the Camp David agreement, a number of Israeli workers who had been earning very high salaries working in the fields staged a hunger strike protesting their loss of livelihood. The public, including Gush Emunim, believed that their protest was economic rather than ideologically motivated. Zvi Yehuda Kook, however, wrote to them saying, "our beloved, holy brothers . . . we are all, all of us with you in your struggle—our struggle."[15] Diplomatic pressures on Israel to withdraw from the West Bank, coupled with messianic expectations, provide believers with a paradigm of the faithful flock commanded as part of the process of their own purification, to resist and even to conquer evil adversaries by military power, firm in the belief that God will not abandon them.

Hence, in the case of expansionism, religious extremism leads to heightened rather than curtailed political involvement. The parallel between Agudat Israel and Gush Emunim is that, regardless of the different significance they ascribe to politics and regardless of their different political styles or goals, both groups deny that society itself is a source of authority, that the voting public can legitimately determine fundamental social policy and appropriate values. In other words, both groups deny basic maxims of democratic politics. Politics is an instrument to achieve goals, not a forum for choosing appropriate goals. When decisions arrived at by democratic processes have been judged as contrary to religious convictions (drafting women in the case of Agudat Israel or limiting Jewish settlement on the West Bank in the case of Gush Emunim), both groups have defended violation of the law—not as a mechanism like civil disobedience, whose purpose is to point out the inequity of the law, but because man-made law has to give way to divine law.

In one respect, no group that has ultimate commitments to a fixed set of values, including even secular liberal humanitarian values, will behave differently. Advocates of separation use this fact as an argument for keeping religion out of politics. No religion, certainly not Judaism, is democratic in the sense that it allows a majority vote to decide what its injunctions ought to be or whether its adherents are bound by its injunctions. Religions only differ from one another in the latitude they accord civil government to reach decisions independently of their conceptions of right and wrong (though whether they choose to or have the power to do anything about it is a separate question). In this respect, Judaism allows a Jewish government rather less latitude than Christianity allows a Christian government, though probably more latitude than Islam, at least Islamic fundamentalism, allows a Moslem government. The question, therefore, is not why Agudat Israel and Gush Emunim are a potential threat to Israel's democratic order, restrained primarily by their minority status in the society, but why the much larger and better-organized National Religious Party does not constitute such a danger.[16]

There are a number of responses to this question. The first is to deny its premise. We are not certain that the NRP, given a large enough vote, would continue to adhere to the rules of the democratic-libertarian game. There are authoritarian, nonlibertarian elements among the NRP leaders who even today seek to limit freedom of speech, and there is probably an even higher percentage of such people among NRP voters. But such elements exist among both leaders and supporters of many other Israeli parties as well. And should the NRP support deviation from basic democratic norms, it would at least, we believe, precipitate an internal fight and a major realignment within the NRP.

Second, the NRP has its own democratic tradition. In its internal operations, the NRP, perhaps more than any other Israeli party, is built on a democratic foundation. When democratic processes are circumvented, and this frequently happens, the party finds it necessary to apologize. Unlike Agudat Israel, it does not revel in its nondemocratic procedures or, like Gush Emunim, have such a fixed ideological program that the group need only concern itself with tactical questions.

Third, and related to the last point, is that lay leaders rather than rabbinical figures control the party. The latter are necessarily more authoritative since they are subject to the temptation to define their statements or have their statements interpreted by others as the voice of God or Torah. The NRP has deliberately relegated rabbinical authorities to roles of secondary importance within the party hierarchy. This leaves the leadership in the hands of professional politicians, who by virtue of their own experiences and propensities are sensitive to voters and naturally seek consensus. We are not suggesting that NRP leaders believe that the voice of the people is the voice of God, but because they rose to leadership in a democratic system they are more likely than rabbinical authorities to be attentive and respectful of the voice of the people. Some, as we shall see, are inclined to attribute a certain sanctity to the voice of the people.

The program of religious Zionism puts great emphasis on Jewish peoplehood and the unity of the people. It also tends toward the pragmatic rather than the romantic. Hence the NRP becomes responsible for and accountable to all the citizens or at least all the Jewish citizens of Israel and even to Jews throughout the world, but it does not reinterpret what people say in *a priori* theological categories suitable to what the romantic wants to hear. This tendency is reflected in recent arguments that both NRP leader Zevulun Hamer (present minister of education) and, contrary to point three, Rav Yehudah Amital (leader of one of the major religious Zionist yeshivot) offered in opposition to Gush Emunim's program of settlement and annexation of the West Bank and to the Israeli conduct of the war in Lebanon. They suggested that even if Israeli hawks and religious ultranationalists were right, their program divided the Jewish people in the Diaspora and in Israel and that this was too high a price to pay for Gush Emunim's goals.

Fifth, unlike Agudat Israel or Gush Emunim, the religious Zionist program is general and amorphous. Party leaders are not clear about what they would do if they did have a majority. Hence, lacking a detailed program to fight for, they are more receptive to what others suggest.

Finally, if one compares the leadership of the NRP and the bulk of its followers with Agudat Israel or Gush Emunim, one is inclined to evaluate them as less religiously committed to their particular brand of religion. With all due respect to the religious integrity of the NRP, we think it is fair to note that they are not quite as committed to "religion" because they are also committed to other aspects of life in the material and cultural realms. This means they are less single-minded, less zealous, and less close-minded. It may handicap them politically in their intraparty or intra-religious camp struggles, but it does make them more suitable partners in a stable political system.

Notes

PREFACE

1. A different conception of the appropriate relations between religion and state and a response from a Jewish perspective to some of the assumptions listed here is Aharon Lichtenstein, "Religion and State: The Case for Interaction," *Judaism* 15 (Fall 1966): 387–411.

CHAPTER ONE: THE MEANING OF JEWISH IDENTITY

1. Simon Herman, *Israelis and Jews: Continuity of an Identity* (New York City: Random House, 1970; copublished with the Jewish Publication Society, Philadelphia), and *Jewish Identity: A Social Psychological Perspective* (Beverly Hills: Sage, 1977).
2. Charles Liebman and Eliezer Don-Yehiya, *Civil Religion in Israel: Traditional Religion and Political Culture In the Jewish State* (Berkeley: University of California Press, 1983).
3. Whereas *dati* literally means "religious," in Israel it connotes a Jew who observes the religious commandments. Since the term "religious" means something else to American Jews, we will use the Hebrew term *dati* to denote an observant Israeli Jew. The American counterpart of the Israeli *dati* is an Orthodox Jew, although there are some American Jews who define themselves as Conservative rather than Orthodox but are quite observant of Jewish law and would, were they in Israel, fall into the category *dati*.
4. For details of the survey results, see Liebman and Don-Yehiya, *Civil Religion*, Ch. 1.
5. George Friedman, *The End of the Jewish People?* (New York: Doubleday, 1967).
6. The significance of religious commitment for a whole host of other indicators of Jewish identity is documented in almost every empirical study of Jewish identity. For a list of such studies, see Charles S. Liebman, "The Sociology of Religion and the Study of American Jews," *Conservative Judaism* 34 (May/June 1981): 17–33.
7. Daniel J. Elazar, *Community and Polity: The Organizational Dynamics of American Jewry* (Philadelphia: Jewish Publication Society, 1976).
8. Ibid., p. 71.
9. Ibid.
10. Ibid., p. 73.
11. Ibid., p. 74.

Chapter Two: Separation of Religion and State in Israel

1. On the constraints imposed on non-Orthodoxy in Israel, see S. Zalman Abramov, *Perpetual Dilemma: Jewish Religion in the Jewish State* (Rutherford, N.J.: Fairleigh Dickinson Press, 1976).

Chapter Three: The "Status Quo" Agreement

1. No mention of the term "status quo" was made in this letter. Apparently it first appeared at the time Ben Gurion presented his government to the Knesset following the first governmental crisis on October 30, 1950. The term was first made part of a formal agreement in the coalition agreement following the elections to the Third Knesset in 1955.
2. David Vital, *Zionism: The Formative Years* (Oxford: Oxford University Press, 1982).
3. The tendency to prevent or resolve political conflicts by refraining as far as possible from reaching any decisions in matters of serious controversy, especially those involving principles, is an accepted method in other countries as well. See, for example, Robert Dahl, *Pluralist Democracy in the United States* (Chicago: Rand McNally, 1967), p. 295.
4. For a discussion of a number of such cases, see S. Zalman Abramov, *Perpetual Dilemma: Jewish Religion in the Jewish State* (Rutherford, N.J.: Fairleigh Dickinson University Press, 1976).

Chapter Four: The Dilemma of Reconciling Traditional Culture and Political Needs

1. Eliezer Don-Yehiya, "Religion and Coalition," in *The Elections in Israel, 1973*, ed. Asher Arian (Jerusalem: Israel Academic Press, 1975).
2. David Apter, *The Politics of Modernization* (Chicago: University of Chicago Press, 1965), p. 25.
3. Robert Bellah and Phillip Hammond, *Varieties of Civil Religion* (New York: Harper and Row, 1980), p. 9.
4. See John Wilson, *Public Religion In America* (Philadelphia: Temple University Press, 1979), for a similar distinction.
5. Clifford Geertz, *The Interpretation of Cultures* (New York: Basic Books, 1973), 238–49, has labeled this the conflict between essentialism and epochalism.
6. Survey data are reported in chapter one of Charles S. Liebman and Eliezer Don-Yehiya, *Civil Religion In Israel* (Berkeley: University of California Press, 1983).
7. Ian Lustick, *Arabs in the Jewish State* (Austin: University of Texas Press, 1980).
8. Ehud Luz, "On the Maccabean Myth of Rebirth," *Hauma* 18 (December 1979, in Hebrew): 44–52.
9. Avshalom Reich, "Changes and Developments in the Passover Haggadot of the Kibbutz Movement," Ph.D. diss., University of Texas, 1972.
10. For the source of this quote and other material of a similar nature, see Liebman and Don-Yehiya, *Civil Religion*, ch. 2.

11. Liebman and Don-Yehiya, *Civil Religion,* ch. 2, and Yael Zerubavel, "The Last Stand: On the Transformation of Symbols in Modern Israeli Culture," Ph.D. diss., University of Pennsylvania, 1980.
12. Liebman and Don-Yehiya, *Civil Religion,* ch. 2.
13. Ibid., for all the original Hebrew sources.
14. Ibid., ch. 3.
15. David Apter, "Political Religion in the New Nations," in *Old Societies and New States,* ed. Clifford Geertz (New York: The Free Press, 1963), pp. 57–104.
16. David Ben Gurion, *Stars and Dust* (Ramat-Gan: Massada, 1976, in Hebrew), p. 134.
17. Amos Elon, *The Israelis* (London: Sphere Books, 1972), p. 294.
18. Apter, "Political Religion."
19. Charles S. Liebman and Eliezer Don-Yehiya, "Traditional Judaism and Civil Religion in Israel," *Jerusalem Quarterly,* no. 23 (April 1982): 57–69.
20. Elon, *The Israelis,* pp. 205–206.
21. Sources in this section, unless otherwise noted, are found in Liebman and Don-Yehiya, *Civil Religion in Israel,* ch. 5 and ch. 6.
22. David Ben Gurion, "Concepts and Values," *Hazut* 3 (1957, in Hebrew): 8.
23. David Ben Gurion, *In the Conflict,* vol. 4 (Tel-Aviv: Hotzaat Mapai, 1949, in Hebrew), p. 12.
24. *Knesset Protocol, 1952* (in Hebrew), p. 910.
25. Reich, "Changes and Developments," p. 393.

CHAPTER FIVE: RELIGIOUS ORTHODOXY'S ATTITUDES TOWARD ZIONISM

1. For a discussion of the background of the religious parties, see Gary Schiff, *Tradition and Politics: The Religious Parties of Israel* (Detroit: Wayne State University Press, 1977) and Eliezer Don-Yehiya, "Origin and Development of the Agudah and Mafdal Parties," *The Jerusalem Quarterly,* no. 20 (Summer 1981): 49–64.
2. On the Edah Ḥaredit and its relationship with Agudat Israel from a very partisan perspective and with important documentary sources, see Isaac Domb, *The Transformation* (London: Hamadfis, 1958). See also Emil Marmorstein, *Heaven at Bay* (London: Oxford University Press, 1969).
3. The best essay on the development of Zionism is Arthur Hertzberg's introductory essay in *The Zionist Idea,* ed. Arthur Hertzberg (New York: Doubleday, 1959). For a historical survey, see David Vital, *The Origins of Zionism* (Oxford: Oxford University Press, 1975).
4. On Kalischer and Alkalai, see Hertzberg and Vital, cited in the previous note, and Jacob Katz, "Tsevi Hirsch Kalischer," in *Guardians of Our Heritage,* ed. Leo Jung (New York: Bloch Publishing, 1958), pp. 209–27.
5. A recent article by Arie Morgenstern, "Messianic Conceptions and the Settlement of Eretz-Israel," *Cathedra,* no. 24 (July 1982, in Hebrew): 52–69, maintains that an almost identical controversy took place at the beginning of the century. The article's implications are quite revolutionary for understanding the beginning of the modern settlement of the land of Israel. If the author is correct, then immigration in the beginning of the nineteenth century by disciples of Rabbi Elijah, the Gaon of Vilna, was undertaken explicitly for purposes of hastening the Redemption and was associated with eschatological expectations in 1840 (later

postponed to 1846). The consequent disappointment resulted in transfer of leadership among the new immigrants to a less mystical, more practically oriented group. This would also help account for the objections to Kalischer and Alkalai by settlers in the land of Israel.

6. On the background and impact of Jewish emancipation, see Jacob Katz, *Out of the Ghetto* (Cambridge: Harvard University Press, 1973). For a comparison of Zionist forerunners and Reform Judaism, see Jacob Katz, "The Jewish National Movement," *Journal of World History* 11 (1968): 267–83.

7. On Hovevei Zion, see David Vital, *The Origins of Zionism*. Yosef Salmon has written most widely on the attitudes of religious Jews toward Zionism and Hovevei Zion in the latter part of the nineteenth century. Of special interest is "The Conflict Between the Orthodox and Enlighteners in Hovevei Zion," *Hatziyonut*, vol. V (Tel-Aviv: Tel-Aviv University Press, 1978, in Hebrew), pp. 43–77.

8. In addition to Hertzberg and Vital, cited above, see a second book by Vital, *Zionism: The Formative Years* (Oxford: Oxford University Press, 1982), which discusses Ahad Ha'am's influence in the early years of the century.

9. Wasserman and other religious antagonists as well as proponents of Zionism are treated in greater detail and from a slightly different perspective in Charles S. Liebman and Eliezer Don-Yehiya, *Civil Religion in Israel* (Berkeley: University of California Press, 1983), where Hebrew sources are cited. Domb, *The Transformation*, contains a variety of anti-Zionist statements issued by religious leaders.

10. For an analysis in English, see Allan Nadler, "Piety and Politics: The Case of the Satmar Rebbe," *Judaism* 31 (Spring 1982): 135–52, and the literature cited in note 2.

11. On Reines and his role in the Zionist movement, see Vital, *Zionism: The Formative Years*. There is very little available in English on this interesting and controversial figure, who was a rebel of sorts on issues of a general Orthodox nature (for example, he favored a form of education for Orthodox Jews that was different from that customary in Eastern Europe). The most comprehensive article on Reines's role as a Zionist leader of Orthodox Jews is Eliezer Don-Yehiya, "Ideology and Policy Formation in Religious Zionism: The Ideology of Rabbi Reines and Mizrahi Policy Under His Leadership," *Hatziyonut*, vol. VIII (Tel-Aviv: Tel-Aviv University Press, forthcoming, in Hebrew).

12. For a biography of Breuer and selections from his publications, see Isaac Breuer, *Concepts of Judaism* (Jerusalem: Israel Universities Press, 1974).

13. Charles S. Liebman and Eliezer Don-Yehiya, *Civil Religion*.

14. There is surprisingly little in English on Rav Kook, given his importance to religious Zionists. His thought is best explored in selections from his writings in Abraham Isaac Kook, *The Lights of Penitence, The Moral Principles, Lights of Holiness, Letters and Poems* (New York: The Paulist Press, 1978).

15. Cited in Liebman and Don-Yehiya, *Civil Religion*.

16. Zvi Yehuda Kook, *L'Netivot Yisrael* (Jerusalem: 1969). On his political importance within Gush Emunim, see Ehud Sprinzak, "Gush Emunim: The Tip of the Iceberg," *The Jerusalem Quarterly*, no. 21 (Fall 1981): 28–47.

17. Kook, *L'Netivot Yisrael*, p. 160.

18. Ibid., pp. 157–58.

19. The relationship between ideology and practice among religious Zionists is more fully developed in the final chapter.

20. On the philosophy of *Torah v'avoda*, see the relevant articles in *Religious Zionism: An Anthology*, ed. Yosef Tirosh (Jerusalem: World Zionist Organization, 1972). For a brief history of Hapoel Hamizrahi and an important selection

of documents from its past, see *Hapoel Hamizrahi: 1925–1935,* ed. Aryeh Fishman (Tel-Aviv: Tel-Aviv University Press, 1979, in Hebrew).

21. Abraham Stein, "By Paths of Peace, Not Force," *Maariv,* September 3, 1982 (in Hebrew).

CHAPTER SIX: RELIGIOUS LEADERS IN THE POLITICAL ARENA

1. For a detailed analysis of the theoretical relations between the authorities, see Stuart A. Cohen, "The Concept of Three Ketarim," *AJS Review,* vol. viii (Cambridge, Mass.: Association for Jewish Studies, 1983).
2. Donald E. Smith, *Religion and Political Development* (Boston: Little, Brown, 1970), p. 7.
3. Menachem Friedman, "The Changing Role of the Community Rabbinate," *The Jerusalem Quarterly,* no. 25 (Fall 1982): 79–99. On the traditional Jewish community, see Jacob Katz, *Tradition and Crisis* (New York: The Free Press, 1961).
4. Charles S. Liebman and Eliezer Don-Yehiya, *Civil Religion in Israel: Traditional Religion and Political Culture in the Jewish State* (Berkeley: University of California Press, 1983).
5. Joseph Lapalombara and Myron Weiner, "The Origin and Development of Political Parties," in *Political Parties and Political Development,* ed. Joseph Lapalombara and Myron Weiner (Princeton: Princeton University Press, 1966), pp. 19–21.
6. Smith, *Religion and Political Development,* p. 124.
7. Gary S. Schiff, *Tradition and Politics: The Religious Parties of Israel* (Detroit: Wayne State University Press, 1977), p. 153.
8. Michael Fogarty, *Christian Democracy in Western Europe 1920–1953* (London: Routledge and Kegan Paul, 1957), p. 6. There is, in some of the European countries (such as Italy), a considerable gap between theory and practice concerning the role of the church in Christian-Democratic politics. See Mario Einaudi and François Gougel, *Christian Democracy in Italy and France* (Hamden: Anchor, 1969), pp. 29, 53–54, 84–87.
9. The best discussion of this topic is found in chapters three and four of Menachem Friedman, *Society and Religion* (Jerusalem: Yad Yizhak Ben Zvi, 1977, in Hebrew).
10. In his subsequent activity, Goren was a disappointment to those who hoped he would contribute to a liberalization or adaptation of *halakha.*
11. Smith, *Religion and Political Development,* p. 85.
12. Liebman and Don-Yehiya, *Civil Religion,* ch. 4.
13. Ben Gurion's position can be found in his speeches to the Knesset, *Divrei HaKnesset, 1951,* p. 1243 (in Hebrew), and in his article "The Eternity of Israel," *The Israel Government Year Book, 1954,* pp. 22–23 (in Hebrew).

CHAPTER SEVEN: THE ANATOMY OF A RELIGIOUS PARTY

1. Giovanni Sartori, *Politics and Party Systems,* vol. 1 (Cambridge: Cambridge University Press, 1976), p. 90.
2. Among 767 Youth Faction candidates to the 1968 NRP convention, more than two-thirds belonged to the intelligentsia (teachers, free professions, students,

rabbis, etc.). The Youth Faction did best in the 1968 party elections in districts with a high proportion of such voters and poorest in areas with a high proportion of new immigrant and Sephardic voters. (See, for example, *Hatzofeh,* October 25 and October 31, 1968, in Hebrew).

3. In 1962, 68 percent of NRP leaders were of Polish and Russian origin and 8 percent of Sephardic origin.

4. Mordecai Bar-Lev, "The Graduates of the Yeshiva High Schools in Eretz-Israel: Between Tradition and Innovation," Ph.D. diss., Bar-Ilan University, 1977, in Hebrew.

5. Asher, Arian, *The Choosing People* (Cleveland: Case Western Reserve University, 1973), and Shimshon Zelniker and Michael Kahan, "Religion and Nascent Cleavages: The Case of Israel's National Religious Party," *Comparative Politics* 9 (October 1976): 52.

6. Arian, *The Choosing People.*

CHAPTER EIGHT: RELIGIOUS EXTREMISM IN ISRAEL

1. On the background to Orthodoxy in the modern era and an elaboration of the ideological typologies listed here, see Charles S. Liebman, "Religion and the Chaos of Modernity: The Case of Contemporary Judaism," in *Take Judaism for Example: Studies Toward the Comparisons of Religion,* ed. Jacob Neusner (Chicago: University of Chicago Press, 1983), pp. 147–64.

2. See chapter five for a more detailed exposition.

3. Charles S. Liebman, "Orthodox Judaism Today," *Midstream* 25 (August/September 1979): 19–26.

4. "Turnover in B'nei Akiva," *Panim Lepanim,* (December 12, 1979, in Hebrew), pp. 12–13.

5. Mordecai Bar-Lev, *"The Graduates of the Yeshiva High Schools in Eretz-Israel: Between Tradition and Innovation,"* Ph.D. diss., Bar-Ilan University, 1977, in Hebrew, pp. 121–22.

6. Elsewhere one of us has argued that this is true of all religion. Charles S. Liebman, "Religious Extremism As a Religious Norm," *Journal for the Scientific Study of Religion* 22 (March 1983): 75–86.

7. Lawrence Kaplan, "Education and Ideology in Religious Zionism Today," *Forum* (Fall/Winter 1979): 25–34.

8. Jacob Neusner, *Method and Meaning in Ancient Judaism* (Missoula, Montana: Brown Judaic Series, Scholars Press, 1979), pp. 123–31.

9. Bar-Lev, "Graduates of Yeshiva High Schools."

10. Ibid.

11. Mary Douglas, *Natural Symbols* (New York: Pantheon, 1970).

12. Bar-Lev, "Graduates of Yeshiva High Schools," p. 415.

13. Charles S. Liebman and Eliezer Don-Yehiya, *Civil Religion in Israel: Traditional Religion and Political Culture in the Jewish State* (Berkeley: University of California Press, 1983).

14. Other reasons account for the fact that one finds little reflection of the rise of religious extremism in the proportion of voters supporting Agudat Israel. While an analysis of voting data takes us beyond the concern of this chapter, we do observe that during the 1970s there was a slow but steady decline in the proportion of total Jewish elementary-school pupils enrolled in schools under Agudat Israel auspices. The reasons stem from the particular age composition of the neo-

traditional world, which was skewed as a result of the Holocaust. That age composition, other things being equal, should have resulted in a sharp decline in political support for Agudat Israel instead of the constant or slightly growing rate of support. Given the very high current birth rates of the neo-traditionalist world, we anticipate a noticeable increase in Agudat Israel's voting strength in the future. Of course, religious extremism may result in an increase in those who define the very act of voting in Israeli political elections as religiously objectionable. The camp that is more extreme than Agudat Israel may also be growing.

15. Quoted in *Nekudah* 42 (December 24, 1982, in Hebrew), p. 5. *Nekudah* is the publication of the Jewish settlements on the West Bank. The statement was quoted approvingly.

16. On the argument that religious extremists in general are the more authentically religious and religious moderates the ones whose behavior requires explanation, see Charles S. Liebman, "Religious Extremism as a Religious Norm."

Index

Abuḥatzera, A., 116, 117, 118
Adaptationism, 121, 126–27
Agudat Israel, 22, 26, 27, 32, 33, 35, 57, 62, 63, 64, 65, 66, 69, 86, 88, 89, 90, 93, 94, 97, 100, 101, 102, 111, 113, 116, 121, 134, 135, 136, 137; and the Council of Torah Sages, 88, 89, 90
Aḥdut Ha'Avodah, 39
Alignment, the, 106, 107, 108, 109, 110, 111
Alkalai, J., 58, 59, 67
American Jews: definition of, 8–10; identity of, 10–14
American Orthodoxy, 12
Amiel, M. A., 67, 68, 69, 70, 78
Amital, Y., 137
Apter, D., 41, 51, 52
Arabs, 16, 48, 108, 116
Ashkenazic Jews, 17, 24, 36, 83, 92, 93, 94, 105, 115, 117
Associated Jews, 11

Balfour Declaration, 65
Begin, M., 18, 27, 40, 115
Bellah, R., 42
Ben Gurion, D., 5, 23, 32, 33, 35, 39, 50, 51, 52, 55, 91, 95, 96
Bible, the, 51–52
Biluim, 60
Blau, M., 62
B'nei Akiva, 123
B'nei Israel, 92
Borochov, B., 49
Breuer, I., 65, 66

Camp David agreement, 114, 115
Canaanism, 5
Catholic church, 8, 80, 87, 88, 90
Chief rabbinate, 20, 36–37, 99
Chief Rabbinical Council (CRC), 18, 36, 37, 83–84, 85, 88, 89, 90–94, 96, 97, 98, 99, 107, 109, 110
Christian Democratic parties, 90, 116
Christians, in Israel, 19
Church model, 80–81
Civil religion, in Israel, 41–56

Commandment of conquest, 75
Compartmentalization, 121, 127
Confrontation approach, 44–45; and Labor Zionism, 48–51, 55, 56
Contributors and Consumers, 11
Council of Torah Sages, 88, 89, 90
Culture, traditional, 41–56, 80–82, 85, 90

Datiim, 3–4, 6, 123
Dead Sea Scrolls, 52
Diaspora, 4, 5, 6, 7, 26, 47, 55, 59, 60, 64, 65, 72, 73, 75, 80, 81, 107, 127
Dietary laws, 32, 122
Discrimination, religious, in Israel, 19
Divorce. See Marriage and divorce law
Douglas, M., 131, 132
Druckman, H., 79

Edah Haredit, 58, 63, 66
Education, 32, 33, 34–36. See also Schools
El-Al, 40
Elazar, D., 11
Eliyahu, M., 94
Elon, A., 54
Emancipation, of Jews, 59
Emunim. See Gush Emunim
End of the Jewish People, The, 5
Exile. See Diaspora
Expansionism, 70–76, 122, 124, 127–28, 133, 134, 135
Extremism, religious, 122–26, 128–29, 133–37

Friedman, G., 5

Goren, S., 92, 93, 94, 97, 99, 109
Government: service model, 41–42, 43; visionary model, 42–44, 46
Governmental service, 22
Group autonomy, 23
Gush Emunim, 76, 79, 85, 94, 106, 108, 109, 114, 122, 127, 133, 135, 136, 137

Ha'am, A., 61
Ha'Aretz, 39, 131
Haggadah, 47, 49, 53

145

Halakha (religious law), 17, 21, 24, 25, 26, 28, 29, 61, 82, 89, 93, 96, 107, 120, 121, 122, 124, 127, 131, 132
Hammer, Z., 18, 137
Hannukah, 46, 47, 49
Hapoel Hamizraḥi, 57, 77
Ḥareydi l'umi, 123
Ḥareydim, 123
Hateḥiya, 114, 115, 116, 133
Herman, S., 1, 4, 6
Herzl, T., 68
Herzog, Chief Rabbi, 91, 92
Histadrut (the General Federation of Labor), 23
Holocaust, 5, 6, 9, 54–56, 76
Ḥovevei Zion (Lovers of Zion), 60

Identity, Jewish, 1–14; basic questions of, 2–3; definition of, in Israel, 3–10; intensity of, in America, 10–12
Ikvita d'meshiḥa (footsteps of the messiah), 70, 71
Independence Day, 52, 75, 94
Informational Guidelines to the Commander, 54
Institutionalized pluralism, 22, 23
Institutionalized religious leaders, 83, 84, 85
Institutional level, of religion and state, 18–23
Integral Jews, 11
In the Camp, 53
Israel, 4, 9, 11, 74, 75, 76, 78, 96, 100, 125; civil religion in, 41–56; national unity of, 29–30, 31, 72, 73, 74, 112, 134; religious discrimination in, 19; separation of religion and state in, 15–30

Jewish Consciousness Program, 18, 53
Jewish identity, 1–14
Jews: American, 8–14; Associated, 11; Contributors and Consumers, 11; Integral, 11; Participants, 11; Peripherals, 11; Quasi, 11; religious (*dati*), 3–4, 6, 123; repudiators, 11; secular, 3–4, 6, 29; traditional, 3–4, 6. *See also* Ashkenazic Jews; Modern Orthodoxy; Orthodox Jews; Sephardic Jews
Judaism, 6, 10, 41, 48, 51, 57, 67, 69, 71, 73, 77, 106, 126, 136; definition of, 2–3, 61; and relation between church and state, 80

Kahana, Rabbi, 115
Kalischer, Z., 58, 59, 67
Kaplan, L., 128

Knesset, 20, 24, 25, 34, 38, 54, 98, 114
Kook, A. I., 63, 67, 68, 70, 71, 72, 73, 74, 75, 76, 77, 78, 90, 91, 115
Kook, Z. Y., 74, 75, 76, 78, 108, 112, 113, 122, 135

Labor Party, 97, 106, 114, 115. *See also* Mapai
Labor Zionism, 48–51, 52, 53, 55, 56, 113
Lavon, P., 55
Law of Return, 106, 107, 109, 110
Law of Working Hours and Rest, 38, 39
Laws: dietary, 32, 122; marriage and divorce, 24–25, 38, 93; Sabbath rest, 24, 26, 38–40
Legislation, religious, 24–28
Leibowitz, Y., 78
Lerner, M., 64
Liberal constitutionalism, 42
Likud, 23, 27, 34, 53, 63, 70, 97, 106, 108, 109, 111, 114, 115, 117
Local religious councils, 20

Mamlakhtiut (Statism), 5, 50–52, 53, 55, 56, 96
Mamzerim, 25, 93
Mapai, 33, 35, 37, 39, 70, 91, 92, 97, 110. *See also* Labor Party
Marriage and divorce law, 24–25, 38, 93
Meir, Golda, 25, 107, 109, 110
Merkaz Harav, 76, 94
Ministry of Education and Culture (Israel), 19, 35, 111
Ministry of Religious Affairs (Israel), 18, 37, 97, 110
Ministry of the Interior (Israel), 19
Mizraḥi, 32, 33, 35, 37, 57, 63, 64, 68, 69, 70. *See also* National Religious Party
Modern Orthodoxy, 121–26, 130, 131, 132, 133
Mohliver, S., 60
Moriah, 64, 65
Moses, 53–54
Muslims, in Israel, 19

National Religious Party (NRP), 20, 26, 27, 37, 57, 86, 88, 89, 90, 92, 93, 97, 99, 100–18, 124, 127, 136, 137; Youth Faction, 101, 102–105, 124. *See also* Mizrahi
National unity, 29–30, 31, 72, 73, 74, 112, 134
Neo-traditionalism, 119–21, 122, 123, 124, 125, 126, 127, 128, 130, 131, 132, 133, 134
Neturei Karta (Guardians of the Wall), 58, 63, 121

Index

New Civil Religion, 53
Nissim, Y., 92, 93, 107
Noninstitutionalized religious leaders, 83, 84, 85, 94
Normative Islam, 80

Organic model, 80–81
Orthodox Jews, 19, 28, 65, 68, 119, 120; attitudes in the Proto-Zionist period, 58–60; attitudes toward Zionism, 57–78. See also American Orthodoxy; Modern Orthodoxy; Jews
Ouziel, Rav, 91, 92

Participants, 11
Passover, 46, 49, 52
Peripheral Jews, 11
Pluralism, institutionalized, 22, 23
Political leaders, relations with religious leaders, 80–83
Politics, religious leaders in, 79–99
Protestantism, 8
Protest voters, 114

Quasi-Jews, 11

Rabin, Y., 107, 110
Rabbinical courts, 20–21, 24, 25
Rabbinical Supreme Court, 98
Raphael, Y., 103
Redemption, 58, 59, 65, 67, 70, 71, 72, 74, 75, 76, 91, 111, 114, 122
Reines, I., 64, 67, 78
Reinterpretation approach, 45, 53, 56
Religion: meaning of, 13; and state, separation of in Israel, 15–30; and status quo agreement, 31–40
Religious: councils, local, 20, 36–37; discrimination, in Israel, 19; education, 19, 21–22, 35, 128–30; extremism, 122–26, 128–29, 133–37; institutions, status of, 36–37; Jews (datiim), 3–4, 6; judicial system, 38; legislation, 24–28; schools, 19, 21–22, 35, 128–30
— leaders, 79–99; relations with political leaders, 80–83; types of, 83–84
Republic, 42
Repudiators, 11

Sabbath rest laws, 24, 26, 38–40
Sadat, A., 114
Satmar Hasidim, 63, 70
Schools, religious, 19, 21–22, 35, 128–30
Secularization, 81, 82, 86
Secular Jews, 3–4, 6, 29

Selectionist approach, 45, 55; and Statism, 50–52, 56
Sephardic Jews, 3, 17, 18, 24, 28, 36, 83, 92, 104, 105, 115, 116, 117, 118
Service model, of government, 41–42, 43
Shapiro, A., 94
Sharett, M., 91
Shavuot, 52
Shrine of the Book, 52
Six-Day War, 94, 106, 111–12, 113, 114, 133
Smith, D., 80, 86, 95
State, and religion: separation of, in Israel, 15–30; status quo agreement, 31–40
Statism, 5, 50–52, 53, 55, 56, 96
Status quo agreement, 31–40
Structured factionalism (of NRP), 101–102
Supreme Court, Israel, 21, 38, 96
Symbolic level, of religion and state, 15–18
Symbols. See Traditional culture

Tami, 116–17, 118
Teitelbaum, J., 63
Tel Ḥai, 50
Toledano, M., 92
Torah, 65, 66, 72, 74, 75
Torah sages (talmudic authorities), 83, 84, 85, 88, 89, 94
Torah v'avoda (Torah and labor), 77
Traditional culture, reconciling with political needs, 41–56, 80–82, 85, 90
Traditional Jews, 3–4, 6. See also Neo-traditionalism
Trumpeldor, J., 49–50

Uganda, 68
United Religious Front, 91, 92
Unity, national, of Israel, 29–30, 31, 72, 73, 74, 112, 134
Unterman, I., 92, 93, 107

Visionary model, of government, 42–44, 46

Warsaw Ghetto uprising, 56
Wasserman, E., 62, 71
Working Hours and Rest Law, 38, 39
World Zionist Organization (WZO), 33, 61, 62, 63, 66, 67, 68, 69, 70

Yad Vashem, 54, 56
Yeshiva, 128–30
Yeshiva Merkaz Harav, 74
Yisraeli, S., 97
Yom Kippur War (1973), 76, 106, 111, 112, 132, 133

Yosef, Ovadia, 92, 93, 94, 97
Youth Faction of the National Religious Party (NRP), 101, 102–105, 124

Zeidman, H., 109
Zionism, 4, 5, 8, 29, 32, 33, 36, 40, 46, 47, 57–78, 81–85, 88, 91, 92, 94, 100, 102–105, 111, 112, 113, 114, 118, 122, 123, 129, 132, 133, 137; and Agudat Israel, 65–66; Labor, and confrontation approach, 48–51, 52, 53, 55, 56; religious, 69–70; as religious messianic phenomenon, 70–76
Zionist Congress, 33